Louisa Jones

The Garden Visitor's Companion

With 185 color illustrations

Thames & Hudson

Acknowledgments

Warm thanks to the many owners and designers who graciously
answered my questionnaires, phone calls, emails and other requests
for information, advice and opinions, as well as those for images from our
ingenious picture researcher, Louise Thomas. Many thanks also to the
efficient editorial team at Thames & Hudson who, for the first time in
my experience with a major publisher, patiently let a fussy author take
full part in the picture selection. Particular appreciation to the talented
art director, Karolina Prymaka, for her beautiful layout. I would like
also to cite some friends and colleagues who have been supportive over
the several years it has taken this project to ripen: in alphabetical order,
John Brookes, Agnès Brückin, George and Marilyn Brumder, Gilles
Clément, Olivier Filippi, Pascal Garbe, Isabelle Greene, Kathryn Gustafson,
Heidi Gildemeister, Martha Kingsbury, Brigitte and Serge Lapouge,
Georges Lévêque, Arnaud Maurières, Tim Richardson, and other young
friends associated with the British Society of Garden Designers.
Not forgetting my long-suffering husband . . .

Louisa Jones
Rousselonge, France, July 2008

On the cover The water parterres of the Tuscan Villa Gamberaia, created over
centuries by the Capponi family, count among the world's most visited and
best-loved gardens. *Jerry Harpur/Harpur Garden Images*

On the half-title page In the garden of Anne-Marie Deloire, ceramic artist,
on the French Riviera.

Frontispiece Heidi Gildemeister's garden in Mallorca, the result of forty years of
love, reflection and hard work, was voted best in Spain in the year 2000.

First published in 2009 in hardcover in the United States of America by
Thames & Hudson Inc., 500 Fifth Avenue, New York, New York 10110

thamesandhudsonusa.com

Library of Congress Catalog Card Number 2008908131

ISBN 978-0-500-51463-4

Printed and bound in China by SNP Leefung Printers Ltd

Contents

Why Visit Gardens?

The man of leisure looks at a garden with serenity,

the man of skill arranges it beautifully,

the superior man enjoys its quintessence.

Zhong Xing, Chinese mandarin (1572–1624)[1]

Places, both urban and natural, are matrices of energy where

thousands of strands of meaning enwrap and enfold the visitor,

who becomes a participant and co-creator of that place.

Gardens are, for many of us, the most special places of all,

filled with myriad threads of experience, emotion and memory,

which combine to make them meaningful . . .

Tim Richardson, English mandarin, 21st century[2]

A very blessed place ...

Gardeners are a curious lot. They want to know what is happening next door, down the road, in the next county or country. 'Twas ever thus: in ancient Nineveh, King Assurbanipal and his queen were already impressing visitors with collections of rare exotics. But curiosity leads to deeper things: in Charlemagne's time (c. 800), monks and scholars travelled from Sweden to Spain to share seeds and skills, thanks to the emperor's programme of horticultural endowment. Garden visiting today has become democratic and global, but all of these motivations are still strong – the desire to discover, compare, seek inspiration, learn and teach, and simply enjoy. Modern garden tourism, like that of Charlemagne's time, may help sustain rural economies, sometimes in unexpected places: poor farmers in the Mekong delta in Vietnam are now organizing garden visits to supplement their incomes by as much as 20 per cent annually. Local craftspeople and restaurants specializing in regional cuisine are participating with garden owners.[3]

Do only gardeners enjoy visiting gardens? The most urban New Yorker includes gardens in trips to Kyoto in Japan, Souchow in China, Florence in Italy, or Great Britain, because gardens are an essential part of the local culture, and above all because their beauty renews and refreshes flagging physical, mental and spiritual energy. Gardeners have always known this, but others are now making the discovery. Sometimes accidentally: in Sri Lanka, a lorry driver delivering bricks to the famous Lunuganga garden of the architect Geoffrey Bawa [opposite] walked around while his cargo was being unloaded, then turned and said to the owner: 'But this is a very blessed place!'[4] And so it is.

Asked what they liked in gardens, French aficionados gave answers like these: 'You open the gate to a garden as you would open the first page of a new book, with the hope of living a moment of happiness in the discovery of a place, a story, a human adventure, a time to dream away from the bustle of everyday life, dream and escape ... a moment outside of time' – thus Thierry

Lunuganga, a very blessed garden by Geoffrey Bawa in Sri Lanka.

and Monique Dronet, of Berchigranges [p. 148]; Bibi Gex, of the Pavillon de Galon, went even further: 'We visit in the hopes of being charmed into following a mysterious call, opening a door onto some new freedom. When you open the gate to a garden, you are never afraid ...'

Great efforts are expended today to keep gardens blessed, in spite of the ever greater numbers of visitors they now welcome. Old gardens which have become icons, like Ryoan-ji in Kyoto [p. 171], Vita Sackville-West's Sissinghurst in England [p. 202] and Claude Monet's Giverny in France [p. 147], are the hardest to adapt for large-scale tourism. Properties originally intended as display parks, such as the Bambouseraie of Prafrance in southern France [p. 70] or the botanical Isle of Mainau in Germany [p. 12], are easier. Gardens and landscapes now enjoy official protection and promotion all over the world. Not only the old ones: while the Taj Mahal remains India's major tourist destination for its harmonious blending of gardens and architecture, the second biggest national attraction is Nek Chand's Rock Garden at Chandigarh [opposite]. Forty years ago, this humble transport official began to collect stones in a little patch of jungle. Working illegally, at night and in total secrecy, he covered several acres before officials found him out and, wisely, decided to encourage him. Thousands of his sculptures are set off by mosaic courtyards, deep gorges and interlinking waterfalls. Over 5,000 people a day now visit the site.[5]

The scale of public projects is getting ever bigger, as with the High Line project in Manhattan, due to be completed in 2010, or the 'marathon' planted roof running for 2 kilometres (1¼ miles) in a public park on the bay in Singapore.[6] The King Abdullah International Gardens, set in the desert of Saudi Arabia, also due to open in 2010, will offer the world's largest garden under a single roof, appealing to a public from all over the world. How to manage crowds without sacrificing quality? In the United States, Longwood Gardens in Delaware [p. 13], created in the early 20th century for the DuPont family, welcomes 15,000 visitors on Easter Sunday alone! The landscape architect Kathryn Gustafson, whose garden-parks can be enjoyed in Amsterdam, Chicago [pp. 24–25]

A detail of the Rock Garden devised by Nek Chand at Chandigarh, in northern India.

and Beirut, flew to Longwood to observe how its management dealt with this influx. She found the overall organization very impressive: 'They had figured things out for all age groups – from the grandmothers to the parents to the kids. Children had little books to take round and things to identify.…The organizers thought a lot about how to involve people. And yet the horticultural collections are phenomenal. It's a very good garden.'

In Europe, an international network called 'Gardens Without Limits' now holds conferences on garden tourism every two years in the city of Metz in eastern France.[7] Among the speakers in 2006 was Countess Bernadotte, of the gardens on the Isle of Mainau in Lake Constance (begun in the early 19th century and opened to the public in 1932 – much to the shock of the neighbouring gentry) [*opposite*]. She welcomes 1.2 million visitors a year, employs 300 gardeners and maintenance workers, and organizes many events and festivals throughout the year for thousands without ever diminishing the interest of the luxuriant botanical collections. Another family venture, in France, is the Château de Villandry near Tours [*p. 52*], famous for its ornamental potager or vegetable garden. Its energetic owner, Henri Carvallo, feels that personal involvement makes all the difference, as long as the family actually lives on the spot.

In France, thirty years ago, Mary Mallet of the Bois des Moutiers gardens [*p. 71*] would invite congenial visitors for tea, while Patrick Sermadiras, owner of the Manoir d'Eyrignac [*pp. 208–9*], might suggest they join him in the pool. Today 90,000 people visit

OPPOSITE Gardens on the Isle of Mainau, in Lake Constance (Germany).

BELOW Longwood Gardens in Delaware (USA) cover 1,050 acres (425 hectares), with twenty outdoor and twenty indoor gardens such as this one.

Eyrignac every year. Sermadiras still welcomes them personally as much as he can. But the old intimacy survives best in smaller French gardens overlooked by tourists, who only think of Normandy, Paris and the Riviera. Agnès Brückin, at the Jardin des Sambucs in the Gard department [p. 68], loves having visitors for 'the pleasure you read on people's faces – elderly people, or children making up a story about the garden as soon as they get past the gate'. She has found no less than four people asleep in bucolic contentment at closing time in various parts of her garden. At Berchigranges in Lorraine [p. 148], Thierry and Monique Dronet saw a visitor who loves grass lie down and kiss it; fifty pairs of shoes left at the gate by people reverently inspired to walk barefoot; and an Englishman proposing marriage to his girlfriend.

How may gardens remain blessed for everyone? The crux of the problem is put very well by Fernando Caruncho, the great contemporary Spanish designer [p. 160]: 'For me, visiting a garden is one of life's greatest pleasures. There is no contradiction in letting one's work be visited. The main thing is to find the threshold, the number of visitors beyond which mystery evaporates. If the spirit goes, the garden will disappear also.'[8]

The child within

The King Abdullah Gardens in Saudi Arabia are being designed to 'illustrate botanical history and show how today's personal and industrial choices determine our future'.[9] Educational goals count more and more in garden tourism. The owners of the Labyrinthe des Cinq Sens at Yvoire, in eastern France near Geneva, estimate that school groups count for about 20 per cent of their 45,000 visitors a year.[10] All the very big gardens now plan special activities for children. Much smaller and just as active, but more inclined towards teaching about natural history, the small Discovery Park of the Vallon du Villaret in central France [p. 113] welcomes 'children from six to eighty'. They are guided along a woodland trail sprinkled with original works of art made on site, meant to be climbed over or through; various games along the track help visitors understand local flora and fauna. Educational goals in gardens seem urgent to the English plant history researcher Sue Eland, who observes that the subjects of botany and horticulture have been dropped by many British schools, colleges and universities.[11] She especially appeals to grandparents to help bridge the gap.

Patrice Taravella, co-designer of the wonderful Prieuré d'Orsan in the Loire region of France [*below*], agrees with this logic. He associates all garden making with the innate creativity of childhood. He himself sought to recreate the warmth of his Italian grandmother's kitchen garden, and he suspects his visitors all have 'their own secret childhood gardens somewhere'. Orsan, he feels, educates people by helping them rediscover the seasonal cycle of growth a garden can provide. Nothing pleases him more than seeing families standing by the formal parterre, planted simply with wheat: 'Grandparents know what it is, their children only sometimes and the grandchildren not at all. So the grandparents explain . . . Some plants can actually close the gap between generations.'

Gardens at the Prieuré d'Orsan in France, created by Patrice Taravella and Sonia Lesot around medieval ruins.

Jean-Paul Pigeat, founder of the International Garden Festival at Chaumont-sur-Loire in France, also insisted on receiving school children because gardens, he felt, should help people of all ages learn how to observe, become aware of the evidence of their senses, and appreciate natural process. This educational dimension of the garden festival is too often forgotten by Chaumont's imitators.[12] But the connection between gardens and childhood may go even deeper: Pigeat, like the British land artist Ivan Hicks, believes that gardens offer 'playgrounds for the inner child',[13] helping to recapture a capacity for wonder too often lost by adults. Hicks offers this experience in his Enchanted Forest at Groombridge in Kent and, in collaboration with the artist Edward James, at Las Pozas in Mexico.

Some styles of gardening, however, have no place for children. In the Japanese tradition, visitor movement is strictly confined to paths and there are no open play spaces, which can make the adaptation of this style to public gardens in the West somewhat problematic.[14] In 2007, correspondents debated the subject of garden visiting as a family activity in the British Royal Horticultural Society's journal *The Garden*. Readers from Luxembourg, bothered by games of hide-and-seek at Sissinghurst [*p. 202*], insisted that 'notwithstanding our sympathy for future garden lovers, we believe young children (and their often too-indulgent parents) can prove disruptive for the meditative and contemplative enjoyment of a haven of peace and quiet.'[15] As a general rule, the more 'planty' the garden, the less it will welcome childhood play.

Why gardeners visit gardens

Stéphane Gaillacq [*opposite*], for many years head gardener at the Château de Chenonceau in the Loire valley (with over 800,000 visitors annually), is also a keen visitor of other gardens. He recalls touring Le Vasterival, one of Normandy's most famous collections and among the first in France to open to the public. Its creator

Stéphane Gaillacq, teaching schoolchildren in the potager of chef Jean Bardet of Tours, in France.

and owner, Princess Sturdza, soon became legendary for her own methods of receiving groups: 'She had test questions and if, after ten minutes, no one could recognize a *Clematis montana*, she took shortcuts and wound up in under an hour. And yet she charged a lot! And if someone walked on her mulch or moved too slowly, she always had in hand a little wand or a light tool and she would tap them smartly on the calf!'

Stéphane himself enjoyed taking people round at Chenonceau and found that visitors could also be curious about the past: 'I much enjoyed showing off our hotbeds made in time-honoured style with horse manure. Today everyone uses modern technology to heat or even practises hydroponic culture, to keep up with the 21st century! At Chenonceau, we showed people how it was done in the 18th. Imagine growing twenty thousand cuttings that way! I thought it was important to show people these methods they can never have known.'

Many gardeners visit mainly to get inspiration for their own gardens. This is perhaps especially true in Britain and countries influenced by the British tradition. Christopher Lloyd, prolific writer and owner of Britain's famous Great Dixter [*pp. 134, 137*], offers sound advice: 'For his health of mind, it is absolutely essential that every gardener should uproot himself from his own patch, now and again, to go and see how other people are doing it, what their problems and interests are, how they approach the subject of gardening and with what result. In this way he keeps himself and his subject in perspective. He gets new ideas for what he would like to grow and how to grow it and he can better assess what, from his own point of view, is worth doing and what seems a waste of effort.'[16] Betsy Brennan, a garden journalist in Australia, agrees that people visit 'to get fresh ideas on design and planting, and tips/information on planning, colour harmonies, maintenance and how other people do it', and implies that a garden is especially interesting if it has growing conditions similar to one's own. The American designer Bunny Williams advises exotic destinations as well: 'The gardens you visit shouldn't be restricted only to those nearby. I may not be able to grow the euphorbias I see on the West Coast, yet I can still learn by seeing how Californians deal with space, arrange plants, and create vistas and interest in their gardens.'[17]

The British tradition stresses plants above all: visitors come to 'steal' ideas (and sometimes seeds and cuttings . . .) for home use. A French gardener has other motivations: 'We visit from a strong desire to discover something new, to enrich our experience, to explore an unknown universe, different from our own.'[18] But in fact these two contrary motivations often intertwine, and new gardens intended for visiting are planned accordingly. A prime example is offered by the twenty-two recently created gardens of the Gardens Without Limits network, covering France, Germany and Luxembourg. They range from minimalist work by the renowned designer Louis Benech at the Château de Pange to the whimsical fancies of young designers trying their skills in a mini-festival at the Citadel of Bitche in Alsace [*opposite*]. One of the best is the 'Garden of Native Flora' at the former home of the European Community pioneer Robert Schuman in Scy-Chazelles: here

Festival garden at the Bitche Citadel in the Moselle, France, part of the Gardens Without Limits network, 2005.

plantings show off varieties developed by locally based but internationally known nurseries such as Lemoine or Simon-Louis, but the management also wants to inform and encourage local gardeners by showing varieties and combinations that do well in local conditions. Pascal Garbe, a garden designer and important advisor for this network, explains that these gardens cater as much to the supermarket checkout cashier as to the international specialist: the most important thing is that each visitor must somehow be able to 'appropriate' the garden in his or her own way. So too says John Brookes, the influential British designer and writer who has received hundreds of thousands of visitors in his garden at

Denmans [*p. 120*]: 'I think the public want to pick up tips sometimes, but more often are simply enjoying a day out in a tranquil place. Throw in a loo and a cup of tea and some sun and they love it, getting lost, holding hands, just being.'

Gardens, nature and art

'In every well-planned garden', wrote Sir George Sitwell in 1909, 'as indeed in every work of art, there are many harmonies of appropriateness – in relation, convenience, proportion or scale, form, colour, historic style – so subtle as to escape individual notice; but these come within the halo of obscurely felt relations, and being fused together rise above the threshold of consciousness in a vague and general sense of ordered beauty.'[19] Garden visiting, like garden making, is both a cultural and a natural activity. Indeed, the current fascination for gardens can be attributed, in part, to our pressing need to redefine human roles with respect to culture and nature. The English historian Tim Richardson cites conceptualist designers like the American Martha Schwartz [*p. 187*] and the Briton Tony Heywood [*p. 184*] for whom all creation is artificial, and 'natural' gardening is hypocritical. They mistrust romanticism, and find that only artifice is honest.[20] But Fernando Caruncho rejects the whole culture/nature split as a false problem: 'We are in nature. I am like a bee, or a beaver, an animal of nature, and I make my gardens in my own natural manner [*p. 160*]. Everything is natural. If man is accepted as part of nature, then everything is natural. If man is not admitted to be part of nature, then everything is artificial. Everything depends on your premise.' Richard Weller, former partner to the Hungarian-Australian conceptualist designer Vladimir Sitta, goes even further. He suggests that what we call 'nature' is often only 'a nostalgic surface image of landscape, a culturally specific selection'. Both he and Sitta consider 'post-industrial pastoral' to be 'one of the most dangerous illusions of our time'.[21] The garden historian John Dixon Hunt, also trying to get beyond conventional categories, sums up 'outdoor place-making' as a blending of 'site, sight and insight'.[22]

This problem seems to be purely Western. Asian cultures take for granted that human life is part of nature and that gardens help restore our harmony with cosmic energy. As a result, even slum dwellers need a bit of greenery for spiritual as much as material nourishment. The Western need to create distinctions – nature/culture, art/nature, high art/low art – is contrary to the whole Taoist tradition. In Asian cultures, garden art has been esteemed for centuries as the equal of poetry and painting. So it was also in Europe from the Renaissance until the 19th century. Gardens were for Sir Francis Bacon the 'greater perfection', superior even to architecture. Today, many Western gardeners seek to reclaim that status. In Britain, Geoffrey and Susan Jellicoe, Brenda Colvin and Dame Silvia Crowe insisted for decades that gardens should be experienced as more than collections of plants.

The British horticultural model has enriched many lives, but its concentration on plants can be narrow – so much so that British expatriates in Italy can be overheard still today complaining that the Italians have no indigenous gardening tradition! Anne Wareham (owner of the garden of Veddw in Wales) objects: 'Visiting a garden with a party of garden enthusiasts, I have been known to make some reflective remark about the effectiveness of an aspect of the design of the garden, only to be met with the kind of pause, silence, and rapid change of subject that greets a lapse of manners in certain circles. Heads down, back to plant naming. . . . Imagine if we transferred our current garden visiting preoccupations to visits to art galleries. The majority of visitors would be there to admire the paints. We would get stickers all over Turner's sunsets identifying each colour, so that we could rush off to the nearest art suppliers to get them. Discussions of paintings would consist of descriptions of paints and their applications, and only fellow painters would visit art galleries at all.' She and her colleagues have now founded a website (www.thinkinggardens.co.uk) to 'encourage and develop a broader, more enquiring attitude to gardens'.[23]

One major problem, for visitors as well as garden-makers, is confusion about description and judgment. For some, garden making is an art which may have good, bad or indifferent results, like any other. But for others, the term 'art' is reserved as a kind of prize, only for the best. The American sculptor Robert Irwin adopts the second approach when he describes his creation at the Getty Foundation in Los Angeles as 'a sculpture shaped like a garden that aspires to be art'.[24] It is in fact the artist who aspires, not the work, and thus his role becomes central. Promoters of conceptualist gardens today often stress the artist's intentions: 'The artist has a set of ideas that are exposed in what is created, and the creation asks questions of the person viewing or experiencing it.'[25] Tim Richardson, a champion of this school, summarizes: 'Conceptualist gardens and landscapes are predicated on ideas rather than plants or the architectural use of hard materials. Such spaces are underpinned by a single concept or visual motif which informs every aspect of the design. The role of the artist or designer is therefore paramount, while the old idea of nature as a legitimate guiding force for design is rejected.' Critics object that all works of art, whatever their medium, should be judged on what they are and not on the aspirations, theories or ideals of their makers. The onus may then shift to the reader, viewer, or in the case of gardens, the visitor. Richardson explores this option also and he has even coined an intriguing new term, 'psychotropia', which he defines as 'place understood not just in terms of location, but also in terms of meaning – its history, use, ecology, appearance, status, reputation, the people who interact with the place, its potential future'. He goes on to claim that 'as garden visitors or owners, I would argue that we are not just passive observers; we are co-creators, and every time we experience a garden, we remake it for ourselves and others'.[26]

Conceptualist gardens ask a lot of visitors: can you enjoy the garden without 'reading the book' first? Today, many visitors find their pleasure enhanced by greater knowledge – part of the educational vocation now so widely attributed to gardens. How may information best be imparted: via accompanying guides, signposts, brochures? Some of the best-known place-makers – the English artist Andy Goldsworthy for example – refuse any on-site commentary and rely on books, magazines or gallery shows of photographs to provide explanations. Others consider that effective communication must be an essential part of the site's original design. Season-long garden festivals often provide a fertile testing ground for both conceptualist experimentation and public response. After Chaumont in France came Lausanne, Stockholm, Métis in Canada [p. 194], Cornerbrook in California and, in 2007, Emo Court in Ireland.

The question 'What is art?' can never be truly answered, but this is nothing new. More interesting perhaps is the growing convergence between garden making and contemporary art. An aphorism attributed to the Scottish artist Ian Hamilton Finlay would have it that 'Gardening is no longer considered an art, but contemporary art is often an inept form of gardening.'[27] The art world has changed a lot since 1968, when the American artist Robert Smithson queried condescendingly: 'Could one say that art degenerates as it approaches gardening?'[28] Smithson focused on entropy, decay and death. The French art philosopher Anne Cauquelin notes that more and more contemporary works include 'live material', i.e. plants. Her definition of an art installation could apply to anyone's home garden: 'arranging objects and individuals in space in such a manner as to make things happen'.[29] The German landscape architects Peter and Anneliese Latz once described their work as 'making time visible', a phrase that can well be applied to a garden.[30]

The work of top level landscape architects like the Latzes allows for the readiest comparisons with contemporary art. Today, however, even conceptual projects on a grand scale may involve horticultural expertise, such as Kathryn Gustafson's work at the Lurie Garden in the Millennium Park in Chicago [pp. 24–25], where the Dutch nurseryman Piet Oudolf did the plantings. Funnily enough, the exhibitions connecting art and gardens held in 2004 at the two Tate galleries in London perpetuated – unknowingly? – the conventional schism between plants and art: Tate Britain was given over to depictions of flourishing, colourful, vital home gardens, whereas Tate Modern concentrated on highly abstract and sometimes morbid creations; nature was excluded except

Overleaf The Lurie Garden, designed by Gustafson Guthrie Nichol Ltd, Piet Oudolf and Robert Israel, forms part of the complex of the Millennium Park in Chicago (USA). In this view it is centre right.

as threatening fantasy, with Smithson's vision still dominating. Outside Tate Modern, the Swiss team Kienast Vogt planted blocks of birches; for Tate Britain, the German-born designer Brita von Schoenaich imagined randomly determined but highly effective annual floral plantings. These sensuous mixes of pattern and pleasure were far more contemporary in conception, spirit and mood than the shows inside.

Today, garden art no longer concerns only landscape architects with budgets worthy of a small nation or an insurance company, nor is it to be found only in public parks. More and more home gardeners strive to add strong design, sculpture and even land art to their horticultural pleasures. Gardening media offer examples and encouragement worldwide. There is also a growing tendency to consult professional garden designers – as a help and not a curb on personal expression. Designers may offer home gardeners not only technical expertise and knowledge of materials but also an educated sense of space, volume and texture likely to produce harmonies that planting alone, for an inexperienced eye, will not achieve. Many of the world's best private gardens emerge from the successful collaboration of two talented people working in harmony – designer and client. Often these creations are accessible to visitors by private arrangement, or on open days. Designers of course may suffer, as all artists dependent on patronage do, from conventional vision or snobbery in the client. At its best, however, such a partnership is an adventure in genuine creativity, 'aspiring to be art'.

Many home gardeners of course prefer to do everything themselves and today cite 'self-expression' as a major incentive for gardening. Scale is not the issue. The French garden designers Arnaud Maurières and Eric Ossart insist that 'landscaping is not a profession but a condition; anyone who gardens, lays out a road, even draws in the sand, is imagining a landscape'.[31] The new ideal, for amateurs as well as professionals, is to work with the hands, the heart and the head all together.

The exchange between creator and visitor can prove unexpectedly fertile. Lynden Miller, an American designer and

'Change of Weather', a temporary festival creation by Latz and Partners for the Federal Garden Show in Munich, Germany, 2005.

horticultural advisor for many public spaces in Manhattan, remembers how she first went to Hidcote, the famous English garden [p. 224], in 1973: 'Graham Stuart-Thomas was still in charge then . . . I was already a painter and it changed my life. I realized I was riveted by the idea of painting with plants. I went on being a painter but I started taking courses at the New York Botanical Gardens where I later taught and designed.'

Thierry and Monique Dronet of Berchigranges [p. 148] have no doubts that visitors are an essential part of the creative process: 'Like musicians, painters, sculptors, the gardener is an artist who needs the reactions of other people to know how he is doing, to express what he feels, to communicate, to exchange, he needs exposure to criticism to make progress. When you choose to live for your art, you are obliged to "sell" it to the public to survive. But that is not necessarily more difficult than going to work in a factory or opening a bakery. Public attention is a bit like fuel. We need the emotions, the encouragement of the public.'

The British historian Janet Waymark resets all the clocks when she concludes: 'The emergence of Land Art has reversed the separation of "garden" and "landscape," and has added a sculptural element to them both . . . Designs for the twenty-first century bind together art, sculpture and Land Art at all levels from domestic gardens to larger landscapes. It appears that in this branch of design, gardens have at last caught up, and are looking ahead.'[32]

Global fusion?

Fashions, plants, and now visitors go round the world faster than ever before. Gardeners worldwide, many of whom travel to each other's continents, share concern about the future of the planet. Growing ecological awareness makes private plots, however small, into fragments of a shared 'planetary garden'.[33] It is gradually becoming recognized, moreover, that Western home gardens have for decades been massively polluting water, soil and air in their pursuit of private Edens. Today, many aspire to reverse this process and make their gardens reserves for biodiversity in both flora and fauna. The general level of concern may still be lamentably low, but few owners today will admit to visitors that they are not entirely 'organic' in their gardening practices – to the point where the politically correct and the merely fashionable may do disservice to real need.

Is there a danger of globalization producing uniformity, spread by the very momentum of green tourism worldwide? The term 'fusion gardening' implies such a universal levelling. Shared ecological responsibility will not perhaps suffice to protect the individuality of garden plots in Sydney, Beijing, New England or Sweden. What forces work against the melting pot or even a mosaic of international styles?

First of all, there is humankind's irrepressible inventivity, which, just as in music, cuisine or language, keeps creating difference. This adaptability and change is a key factor in the basic logic of evolution, so that even when fusion occurs, new individuality may emerge. In 2004, the international designer Peter Wirtz described what was then happening in his native Belgium: 'In this small country where much garden making is fairly recent, where two cultural communities offer a crossroads for multiple influences (Latin, French, German, English, very little from the Netherlands), this very collision of cultures has produced a great freedom and a bubbling over of creative energy. … It has led to very strongly defined individual initiatives, especially in landscape design.'[34]

Another protection comes from the deliberate choice of many gardeners, professional and private alike, to create work which is inspired by each site's unique logic and history. This is a complete reversal of 20th-century modernist and postmodernist trends. Today, most international designers would concur with Peter Latz [p. 27], who proclaims: 'In my projects I am always interested in the "genius of the place" rather than in the genius of my office. Even motorways or industrial wastelands can be filled with a new spirit and can be made worth living by keeping visible the spirit of the existing site. Landscape and open space contain a wealth of information layers.'[35] Some compare land to a palimpsest – a manuscript half erased to be written on again, keeping traces of all earlier versions. Ecological awareness converges seamlessly with this approach based on a close reading and deep understanding of local resources. Gardeners with an educational vocation try to communicate such site knowledge and memory to visitors.

These concerns inevitably raise issues of local identity for both residents and visitors. The Irish International Garden Festival founded in 2007 took as its theme 'Roots – gardens that

evoke a sense of belonging'. Many public works today are commissioned to affirm a particular image associated with local identity, with often controversial results, as with Vladimir Sitta's 'Garden of Australian Dreams' at the National Museum of Australia in Canberra [*opposite*]. For the Australian garden historian Richard Weller, 'landscape is fabric and fabrication in which natural and synthetic threads form new materials and new identities – hybrid products'.[36]

Projects linked to local identity raise the question: to what extent should gardens and landscapes be lumped together? Visitors who are themselves garden makers know that the rapport between gardens and the world outside may be multiple and complex – separation, melding, borrowing, distillation, imitation, parody, metaphor . . . The list is endless. International travellers encounter deep cultural differences. People from industrialized, densely populated Northern European countries often regard the more sparsely inhabited Mediterranean countryside of southern France, Spain and Italy as one big garden. These agrarian landscapes have indeed been carefully tended for millennia, and the countryside, where still unspoiled, presents wonderful landscape panoramas that extend private gardens. In built-up areas like the Riviera, however, gardens survive as islands of greenery in the midst of urban sprawl, comparable to oasis gardens of North Africa in barren or desert settings, or parks creating artificial wilderness in industrial parts of the Netherlands. In these cases, gardens and landscape are at odds with each other.

In the Americas or Australia, where countryside is vast, garden and landscape may once again go their separate ways. The garden model is often the settlement, another kind of oasis, an island of civilization imposed on an often hostile natural setting. When 'wilderness' is experienced as seductive, it has often engendered settler myths of 'virgin' territory, magnificent, open, empty space. Travellers from Australia, South Africa or the Americas sometimes feel claustrophobic in small-scale settings like Provence. Japanese travellers have yet another

Vladimir Sitta's 'Garden of Australian Dreams' at the National Museum of Australia in Canberra.

perspective: Europe and America may to them seem equally 'grandiose'; only in small-scale Japan can landscape, garden and nature form a single ideal 'of grace and delicacy', since 'the country itself is a big garden delicately and exquisitely finished by the hand of Nature, the Divine Artist, in one of her most gracious moods'.[37] The ideal of landscape miniaturization in even the tiniest garden seems more spiritual to Asiatics than Western 'representation', which keeps scale life-size – or larger! Such cultural preconceptions, often unconscious, may affect the most sophisticated travellers.

The business of tourism

The budding garden tourist industry has difficulty dealing with cultural ambiguities and hybrids. For promoters, the question of garden or landscape comes down to commercial categories: should gardens be grouped with monuments and cultural resources? Or do they belong with sports, hiking and other outdoor opportunities? Nothing reveals our Western confusion over nature and culture better than this advertising dilemma.

Garden tourism is growing fast. In 2004, a study claimed that 61 per cent of gardens open to the public worldwide were already affiliated with a tourist organization.[38] Here as in other domains, the conversion of a private passion into a business venture offends some and tempts others, depending on the motivations and sometimes on the scale involved. France offers a particularly interesting example, insofar as gardening fever has taken over the nation intensely but fairly recently, involving all types of gardens and contexts. Surveys in 2007 revealed that 89 per cent of French homes had some sort of garden, even if just a window box or balcony, and 38 per cent grew some of their own vegetables.[39] Plant fairs have mushroomed in the most remote areas. But learning what to plant is not the only, nor even the main, stimulus for the new enthusiasm. A Ministry of Culture document concludes: 'More than a fashion, the garden in France today is a way of life and new gardeners are moved by reasons that are both decorative and sociable: growing ecological awareness, the desire to live harmoniously with nature, to put down roots literally, and to express their own creativity are just some of the factors stimulating this new national passion.'[40]

Plants are important but not central to a generation of French gardeners looking for much more than a casual leisure activity. France has no experienced National Gardens Scheme or National Trust to help and inspire those who want to open their gardens to the public, however: support comes almost uniquely from government organizations that offer opportunities and guarantees (but may also impose conservative uniformity and administrative lethargy). Historic gardens were the first to benefit, understandably. Many owners were already engaged in soliciting architectural listings, and château parks are easier to inventory than small home gardens. The Loire valley and Normandy were naturally pioneers, having already many well established gardens, in the former linked to historic châteaux, in the latter to English connections. Today, however, other regions are coming alive with small, newer home gardens, slowly being awarded the new government label of *jardins remarquables*. Among the most creative gardens in France today – and hardest to find – are those made by a younger generation for whom gardening has become a major life choice. Working on a shoestring and often in remote country areas, these owners have imagined a wide range of original, highly personal gardens.

Township or tourist offices may be the last to understand what the Mekong delta farmers already know – the potential of garden tourism for declining rural economies, not just as window-dressing or postcard fodder but as a legitimate use of land resources. There are some notable exceptions: the small city of Cahors in the south-west with its municipal *jardins secrets* [*p. 35*]; the department of the Moselle, which fully supports the Gardens Without Limits programme; a developing network in Picardy mixing public and private funding;[41] and the Gard department, offering an unusual diversity of gardens with a programme which may well come to serve as a model for other regions [*pp. 55, 68*].[42] But guidebooks, while they provide a certain amount of information, regularly omit the names of landscape architects and designers as being too specialized to interest readers. Imagine if the same discretion were applied to architects!

All of this is likely to change fast, part of an overall evolution in French country life generally. Garden tourism easily adapts itself to current educational, ecological and 'alternative' movements. This is true even at the international level: the experts at Metz suggest a growing convergence between worldwide trends in travel and what garden owners want to offer:[43] heritage sites, natural beauty, human life and activities; themes appealing to small groups with a common interest and affinities; personal contacts with local people; not just relaxation and entertainment. Many today feel that the personal, unstructured exchanges that gardens allow between visitors and owners create community ties and understanding and tolerance among people of different origins. Gardeners exude good will, as everyone knows. Never mind that they are also capable of the most awful rivalries and snobberies, thereby sharing the foibles of human nature with the rest of the population. The ideal remains what the English landscape architect Russell Page proposed to garden owners fifty years ago: 'Remember that one of your aims must be to lift people, if only for a moment, above their daily preoccupations. Even a glimpse of beauty outside will enable them to make a healing contact with their own inner world. Nor must you ascribe such an idea to sentimentality. It is one most valid reason and justification for gardens and for gardeners.'[44]

One of the twenty-five imaginative 'secret gardens' made in recent years by Patrick Charroy and his team of municipal gardeners for the historic centre of the town of Cahors, France.

Ten Questions for Ten Styles...

'What do you look for when you first enter a new garden?', I asked three friends. The first, an artist, replied: 'I look for the telling detail that pulls the whole scene together – a triangular stone set just here, on that wall! Or a candle cypress tree half way up the hill.' The second, a writer, said : 'I want to know who worked on this ground, with what goals, what feelings.' The third, a horticulturalist, said, 'I want to explore the plant associations, see what grows well in this climate and soil, to enjoy the colours and moods.'

Each reader will have different responses to gardens visited. But why not seek pleasure for the understanding as well as the senses; why not engage curiosity as well as the eye and the nose? In what follows, ten questions are proposed for each of ten different types of garden. Each question is amplified with suggestions of things to look for and think about. My aim is not to dictate and circumscribe, but to enhance your awareness and enjoyment, to point up nuances in the art of garden making, to help sharpen perceptions. I have tried also to share the accumulated experiences of previous garden visitors in similar situations; their voices are heard in the selected quotations.

The ten garden types are simply a point of departure. They are neither complete nor mutually exclusive: creative garden makers keep reinventing them. The designer Russell Page wrote: 'Where I have worked well the garden will be content to be itself and bear no obvious label.'[1] The best advice I would offer personally is to take a garden on its own terms: don't judge a cottage garden by the standards of a château park, or a minimalist garden by its plant collections.

The next stage is to look further into garden history, to learn to distinguish period styles, for example, or to recognize and understand the work of individual talents . .

Ten Questions for Historic Gardens

A garden such as that of Lante is a world-possession, and the builder of it like a great poet who has influenced the life of thousands, putting them in touch with the greatness of the past, lifting their thoughts and aspirations to a higher level, revealing to them the light of their own soul, opening their eyes to the beauty of the world.

Sir George Sitwell, *On the Making of Gardens*, 1909

What I like in gardens is that thickness of accumulated time, that passion, all those decisions being made about something which is not a project but a place . . . My profession is to help places continue to exist. Every place is historic.

Pascal Cribier, French landscape architect

What was the original purpose of these gardens? Was it to affirm power or status, allow symbolic representation, receive distinguished guests, encourage religious emotion or meditation, provide pleasure gardens next to a hunting lodge, serve as a country retreat for courtiers or city elites? Perhaps this was the country seat of landed gentry? If the property's main vocation was agricultural, are its productive parts (fields, vineyards, vegetable gardens, orchards) separated from an ornamental park, hidden away, part of a distant view, or proudly displayed all around, as with many Tuscan villas? Do you have access to documents which tell about life in these gardens when first created and at later periods? Does the work done on them today aim at period restoration, renovation, or 'reinvention', which the historian Marie-Christine Labourdette defines as 'work which evokes the memory of a place using innovative forms'.[2] The gardens of Valloires in Picardy, in France [*p. 131*], and Alnwick Castle in Northumberland, in England [*p. 51*], are famous examples of recent 'reinventions'.[3]

Parterres at the French châteaux of Vaux le Vicomte (OPPOSITE) and Versailles (BELOW) provide long vistas linking majestic façades to far horizons. Both were designed by the architect André Le Nôtre. Vaux (1656–61), created for Louis XIV's finance minister Nicolas Fouquet, so impressed the King that he had its owner arrested, then hired Le Nôtre himself. Statuary and even trees were moved from Vaux to Versailles, where palace and park were designed to pay homage to the monarch's power. They have undergone many changes since.

Do the gardens date from the same period or periods as the architecture? Old gardens often survive because of their association with an important monument. Perhaps several different periods are evident in both buildings and gardens. Do successive styles overlap here? Is the mix contrived or happenstance, harmonious or disruptive? Do you like it? Has one period style in particular been featured in restoration work as more 'authentic' than others? The designer Pascal Cribier, who often works on historic properties, has said: 'A French 17th-century façade can look down on gardens mixing several styles with no conflict whatever. I am constantly opposing a perfectly false idea of historic authenticity.' The historian Michel Baridon suggests that we make the most of what we have: 'We are here in the domain of art and the history of styles, a domain one enters with the desire to learn, to understand the past and to appreciate the best of what it has bequeathed us.'[4]

The elaborate parterres of the Villa Lante at Bagnaia (Italy) were designed by Giacomo Vignola in 1573 and much admired by the French writer Michel de Montaigne in 1581. Today Lante is still considered the best-preserved Italian garden of its period (see also pp. 232–33).

Are there visual ties connecting the buildings and the gardens?
Whether created together in the same period or redesigned later on, do they now form a single unit, so that the lines and volumes of the park echo those of a façade? Were avenues, *allées* and parterres intended to be seen also, or mainly, from windows, a balcony, an upper storey? Is the land flat or steeply sloped, perhaps terraced, so that you cannot grasp the whole design from the house? Are there thematic details, in sculpture perhaps, common to both house and garden? Are the plantings strongly architectural? If the gardens are a self-contained world apart from the residence, how is the transition managed between dwelling and garden? Is there a triumphal arch for public, ceremonial access, or a small, secret but enticing entry, or perhaps both?

What is the relationship between the gardens and their setting?
Were the gardens originally inspired by the site and designed to suit it, or imposed upon it through extensive earthworks which changed the topography (marshes drained, slopes regraded, etc.)? Is the garden part of an architectural grouping that goes beyond this property, as with town courtyards, cloisters, or parks which connect a château to the village church? Is it completely enclosed with no view but the sky, as in many Islamic examples? Or does the dome of the sky stretch over a vast perspective? Can you see the horizon line, down long avenues or from high viewpoints? If there is a view, is it edited, framed by trees or buildings, or the last in a series of carefully staged planes? Are the gardens a discrete foreground for a dramatic panorama, do they melt seamlessly into their setting, or is the distant landscape merely a backdrop for a magnificent garden?

ABOVE AND OPPOSITE The gardens of the Villa d'Este at Tivoli (Italy), designed by Pirro Ligorio and constructed in 1560–75 on a steeply terraced hillside, are linked to the villa by a central axis and complex symbolism. Yet their overall design remains mysterious, allowing for the constant discovery of hidden places. Cascades, rockeries and grottoes are at once natural and highly contrived, theatrical settings for visitors to explore. Among the gardens' many pleasures is the music provided by various fountains, including a water organ.

Is the garden's layout formal or 'natural', clearly visible from a dominant point of view, or slowly unveiled, full of surprises?

Is the layout mainly composed of straight lines and right angles? Is the design symmetrical – or made to appear so through visual tricks? Perhaps paths are 'serpentine', progressing along generous curves which disappear between clumps and groves (the 'landscape' style)? Or again, perhaps the plan is abstract and geometric but deliberately asymmetrical (modern design, mid-20th century)? Perhaps the formal parts are also productive – as in vegetable gardens and vineyards? To explore this garden, do you follow a single established itinerary? Have one or several pre-arranged viewpoints been organized to make you stop and look? If the visit is laid out for you, who planned it? Was the itinerary part of the original plan, or something conceived for today's visitors?

BELOW The Vigeland Sculpture Park in Oslo (Norway) was designed in the 1920s as a showcase for the sculpture of Gustav Vigeland. As in its baroque models, the formal, geometrical layout is meant to be clear from a distance, often seen from above, although groves of trees on either side may contain more intimate surprises.

OPPOSITE At Isola Bella, on Lake Maggiore (Italy), an extravagant baroque garden dating from 1650–71 covers an entire island. Each of its terraces, wedded to natural rock formations, affords different but equally dramatic views of a magnificent setting. Surrounding land affords in turn multiple viewpoints on this amazing ship-like garden.

What is the role here of sculpture and objects like urns, vases and pots? Do they serve mainly to echo the architecture or are they important in their own right? Sir George Sitwell wrote about Italian villa gardens: 'It is not only that the statues will set off the garden . . . the garden will set off the statues, crowning them with a garland of beauty they could not have elsewhere.'[5] Are artefacts simply accents blending with a conventional décor, or highly personal creations carefully selected and sited? Are they individual or grouped? Are they numerous? Are there too many of them, producing a cluttered impression? What materials are they made from – local? rustic? precious and imported at great cost? Is their staging obvious, decorous, mischievous, playful, boring, breathtaking, minimalist? Are their shapes and colours uniform, well matched among themselves and to the colours and textures of paths and walls? Are the people who made them famous, and have you seen their work elsewhere?

The gardens of the Generalife in Granada (Spain), on the hillside opposite the Alhambra, illustrate the intricate subdivision of space found elsewhere in Moorish art in a succession of intimate courtyards with lush plantings and fountains. In the Patio de la Acequia, seen here, water rather than sculpture provides the central focus.

RIGHT AND BELOW In 1924, after creating
legendary gardens at Hidcote Manor in
England (see pp. 224–25), Lawrence Johnston
began designing this winter residence,
Serre de la Madone in Menton (France).
Statuary here provides focal points in the
classical manner but shares an exceptional
harmony with setting, plantings and
garden structures.

How were the plants chosen? Are they specifically related to the history of this place, generally evocative of a vague vision of the past, linked to current creation on this site, or simply part of a standard décor? Are their origins and history interesting in their own right, perhaps as part of a horticultural or botanical heritage? Are they perhaps even the main reason for the existence of this garden, as in old arboreta and botanical gardens? If so, is the garden famous because it offers a great diversity of species, or because it has extensive collections of just one or two (peonies, roses, or rhododendrons, for example)? Are flowers or foliage most important here? If architecture dominates, are the plants limited to a very simple range of clipped greenery – yew or box – used mainly for hedging and edging? How are the plants grouped – by mass, colour, texture, successive heights? Is seasonal change and annual growth considered an asset, or is the design intended to remain as immutable as possible?

The Great Garden of the palace of Het Loo at Apeldoorn in the Netherlands was laid out between 1686 and 1695 for Stadhouder William of Orange-Nassau and his wife Mary (by the time it was finished, they were rulers of Britain and Ireland). The decorative motifs of its embroidery parterres have been filled in with different colours of sand, as was often done at that time. Courtiers' costumes also enlivened these essentially green gardens.

Biddulph Grange in Staffordshire (England), a Victorian garden, links high colour and exoticism, here in its much-loved Chinese garden. In the mid-19th century, plant hunters collected shiploads of eastern treasures, such as bamboos, maples, and rhododendrons from the Himalayas. The plants here tell their own story of exotic plunder.

How is colour used in this garden? Is there a subtle mix of foliage tones, a well-orchestrated floral display, an explosion of bright colours? Is each section different? Is there harmony between the buildings, permanent plantings and seasonal accents – perhaps bedding plants (annual flowers), deciduous foliage, vegetables, or a summer festival? Is one colour dominant, as in the white gardens of Sissinghurst [p. 202]? Is there strong seasonal variation (as in a rose garden or an arboretum with autumn colour)? Formal gardens are often essentially green, and the novelist Edith Wharton in her famous book on Italian villa gardens of 1904 warns her readers that they can achieve real 'enchantment' using elements 'as dull and monotonous as a mere combination of clipped green and stone work'.[6] Many historic gardens of course served as a setting for grand festivities and took their colour from the costumes of people regularly attending them.

What role does water play in this garden? Are there fountains – grandiose or intimate? still pools reflecting the changing sky? rills and canals as in Islamic gardens? picturesque cascades imitating the wildness and energy of nature? What characteristics of water are emphasized here – its capacity to catch light, as at Versailles? to suggest shadowy depths, as in certain Japanese gardens? Is it meant to be heard at a distance? Is there technical information available about its source, conservation, pumping, recycling perhaps, both in the past and today? Is there a sea view? Water can be the soul of a garden. Colette, visiting the ancient Roman/ baroque Gardens of the Fountain at Nîmes in southern France, wrote in 1910: 'A whole garden of reflections is spread out there below me, turning, as it decomposes in the aquamarine water, dark blue, the violet of a bruised peach, and the maroon of dried blood. Oh beautiful garden and beautiful silence, where the only sound is the muted plashing of the green, imperious water, transparent and dark, blue and brilliant as a bright dragon.'[7]

How is this historic property used today? Who owns, manages and maintains it? Is it open only occasionally, or is it a major tourist site? Does it now mainly exist as a romantic vision of the past, postmodern pastiche, minimalist re-creation, or an exercise in theme gardens? Does it house botanical collections, contemporary art exhibitions, a zoo, outdoor theatre, regional crafts shows, plant fairs, fencing demonstrations, or something else entirely? What seasonal events entice the public through its gates? In India, the designer Françoise Crémel set the scene for evening events in the family gardens of the Maharaja of Jodhpur by painting selected internal walls with phosphorescent paint, an effect echoing traditional moon gardens.[8] In France, the Panouse family has transformed two family properties into medieval theme gardens with zoos. The Vicomte explains: 'We have welcomed more than 17 million tourists in this place where I grew up ... Tourists help me keep alive these places that I love, but in more than just the obvious economic sense. They give a meaning to my work and to the work of those who help me.'[9]

Owners of Alnwick Castle in Northumberland (England) once commissioned designs by 'Capability' Brown. In recent years, their descendants asked the Belgian architects Jacques and Peter Wirtz to help design spectacular neo-baroque water gardens. The new park's huge success has changed the life of the entire region.

TWO VIEWS

Indeed any one that is just come from seeing the Buildings in *France* and *Italy*, is apt to have but little Taste, or Attention, for whatever he may meet with in the other Parts of the World. However I must except out of this Rule, the Palace of the Emperor of Pekin, and his Pleasure-houses; for in them every thing is truly great and beautiful, both as to the Design and the Execution; and they struck me the more, because I had never seen any thing that bore any manner of Resemblance to them, in any Part of the World that I had been in before.

Letter from Jean-Denis Attiret, S.J. (1702–68), to M. d'Assaut in Paris, 1 November 1743[10]

At One South Coast Place in Costa Mesa, California, the gesture, in its relationship to the entrance, is a form derived from the French Renaissance . . . Typically the French gestures are designed from the inside out . . . With parterres, the spaces become important because of the richness of the surface treatment. They are not defined by walls; they are rugs. They do not have to be elaborate, but they must be of the surface and strong. Chenonceau's parterres are equal to a tremendously dramatic architectural siting over the river. French gardens at the Château de Cheverny, Vaux-le-Vicomte [*p. 41*] and Villandry [*opposite*] also demonstrate the power of a worked surface. These are some of the most powerful gardens ever created.

Peter Walker and Cathy Deino Blake, 'Minimalist Gardens without Walls',
in *The Meaning of Gardens*, 1991[11]

The Loire valley Château de Villandry,
one of France's most visited gardens for
its famous vegetable terraces, also offers
parterres symbolizing love. Designed in
the 1920s though inspired by Renaissance
models, they illustrate the 'power of a
worked surface' admired by the modernist
Peter Walker.

Ten Questions for Cottage Gardens, Grandmothers' Gardens, and 'Jardins de Curé'

Little strips in front of roadside cottages have a simple and tender charm that one may look for in vain in gardens of greater pretension.

Gertrude Jekyll, Wood and Garden, 1899[12]

I gradually came to know the cottagers and their gardens for miles around, for these country folk had a knack with plants. . . . I would be given cuttings from old-fashioned pinks and roses which were not to be found in any catalogue, and seedlings of plants brought home perhaps by a sailor cousin – here was a whole world of modest flower addicts.

Russell Page, The Education of a Gardener, 1985[13]

Where is the garden with respect to the house? English cottage gardens sit proudly between the street and the dwelling, easily seen by passers-by who admire their 'hollyhocks, lavender and roses round the door'.[14] Gables and gates are part of the romantic picture. The French *jardin de curé* (priest's garden) is often compared to the English cottage garden but is tucked away behind the house, a private haven and escape from outside stress. 'Grandmothers' gardens' are often made today by adults remembering childhood country holidays, who translate this nostalgic mood into a weekend retreat. Like their model, they may be hidden, even from the house, visible merely as a glimpse of blue shutter or chimneypot through leafy bowers. Never far away, however, for the garden's herbs are needed in the kitchen. All these variations on the type tend to be small and densely packed.

PREVIOUS PAGES
LEFT Urbane women gardeners like Cali Doxiadis may still enjoy grandmotherly styles in country settings – here Corfu, Greece – happy in the continuity from generation to generation.

RIGHT A very new example, the Jardin des Mille et une Fleurs, created with her own hands by Maria Cancelli in the Gard (France).

On the French Riviera, the garden of La Pomme d'Ambre was made by Nicole Arboireau and her husband, with occasional help from her granddaughter, as a magical world of its own on a steeply terraced hillside. Nicole established a local grandmothers' garden network to save heirloom plants and wrote a book about it, *Jardins de grands-mères*.

In the 1950s, at East Lambrook Manor in Somerset (England), Margery Fish adapted the cottage style to postwar needs, still specializing in lush floral variety but promoting, through her books, the cause of disappearing perennials. A clearly visible path leads up to the front door.

Are the shape, size, boundaries and scale of the garden hard to read?

Cottage gardens have clear boundaries insofar as their space is defined by the road, the house, and neighbours' walls. They give onto the outside world, over a fence or hedge. Within these limits, however, all is 'haphazard luxuriance'.[15] In the self-contained, more private versions, abundance becomes all-enveloping, blurring boundaries, volumes and contours. Very popular today, this style owes much to the influence of the 18th-century French novelist Jean-Jacques Rousseau, who describes an ideal garden, much copied, so luxuriant that notions of scale and depth are lost in happy confusion. French miners' yards also play with scale by including miniatures such as an Eiffel Tower or steamship, in trick perspective.[16] With or without views beyond, such gardens become worlds apart, intermingling inner and outer visions, dream and reality . . .

What are the owner's favourite colours, and how are they assembled?
In bright dabs haphazardly mixed, in orchestrated patterns,
carefully graded progressions, or deliberately violent contrasts?
Do they follow current fashions, or some internal logic of their
own? Shutters and fixtures may be painted a single colour –
usually bright – to create some kind of unity where plantings
might seem a jumble.[17] Colour has always had great emotional
impact, and grandmothers' gardens have immediate emotional
and sensuous appeal. They are often half-shady, so that colour
varies with changing light throughout the day. Colette admired
the garden made by her mother, Sido: 'The whole warm garden
fed on golden light, with flickers of red and violet; but I cannot
say if this red, this violet results from a deep feeling of happiness
or from a purely optical bedazzlement.'[18]

Where did the plants come from? Does the gardener prefer common
wildflowers, garden centre hybrids, rare finds, or everything all
at once? Simple or double flowered varieties? Heirloom or recent
horticultural creations? Are plants part of a carefully arranged
picture, or do they take you – and sometimes the gardener – by
surprise? Are the treasures self-sown gifts from heaven, exchanges
with neighbours, or souvenirs of far countries?[19] Are there bulbs
for all seasons? A mix of flowers with fruit, vegetables and
medicinal plants, on the ground, on walls and in hedges? George
Eliot's ideal garden was 'a charming paradisiacal mingling of all
that was pleasant to the eyes and good for food ... You gathered
moss rose one moment and a bunch of currants the next; you
were in a delicious fluctuation between the scent of jasmine and
the juice of gooseberries; the crimson of a carnation was carried
out in the lurking of the neighbouring strawberry beds ...'[20]

Grandmother Doudou Bayol in Provence
(France) gets her plants from holiday travel,
neighbours' cuttings, seeds sown by the
wind and birds. Her parents were market
gardeners and she proudly calls this a
peasant garden. Her husband, an artist,
often paints it, and she also runs his gallery
– in the garden.

Are there straight lines or other formal elements? The traditional cottage garden has a clearly visible path, not necessarily straight, connecting its gate to the front door. Today's French *jardin de curé* often features two lines, perhaps box-edged, intersecting at right angles to form a cross around a symbolic pool or fountain. Sentimental historians consider this feature conducive to meditation and link it to old monastery gardens, though the style probably owes more to 19th-century Romanticism. Genuine grandmothers' gardens are open to everything – curves, lines, completely unruly vegetation, whatever the owner may prefer, including fanciful topiary in all shapes and forms. Often cited is the compulsive husband who mows or prunes anything spoiling any edge or line. Fanciful irregularity, like colour, is often deemed a feminine attribute.

Who works in this garden? English cottages, according to the historian Anne Scott-James, quickly became favourite dwellings among villagers of all classes, including poor but independent gentlewomen such as Jane Austen and her sister. In such cases a servant might do the actual gardening. Similarly, French priests are depicted praying, walking and meditating rather than actually gardening, though of course there were exceptions. Upper-class women gardeners like Australian-born Elizabeth von Arnim,[21] married in 1891 to a German nobleman, had to fight for the privilege of getting their hands in the dirt. The nostalgia so often associated with this style of garden turns on an ideal harmony between human work and the earth's bounty, and this is hard to experience vicariously. Most owners of such gardens do at least some of the work themselves. Those who prefer humour to romanticism fill odd corners with eccentric constructions and assemblages which usually include places for repose, such as benches and arbours.

Anne-Marie Grivas and her husband worked hard together to create this refined country garden in a suburb of Paris (France), particularly rich with spring bulbs and cascading roses. Meandering paths and pergolas make the plot seem much bigger than it is, hiding the house from view.

Does this garden comply with current tenets of 'good taste'? A miner
participating in a village garden competition was asked to remove
his miniature windmills, painted tyres, a tortoise made from a
plastic dishpan and a fake well from his plot, leaving only lawn,
hedge and flowers. He was devastated.[22] Eric Ossart, head gardener
for many years at the International Garden Festival of Chaumont
and largely responsible for creating the Chaumont style in planting,
took inspiration from French grandmothers in his preference
for vital exuberance, playful readings of space and bright colours.
The results sometimes seemed garish and tasteless to conservative
visitors, especially when garden gnomes were added . . . But as
Ossart's partner, Arnaud Maurières, put it: 'Generosity counts for
more than good taste in gardening.' So dahlias, amaranths, cannas,
marigolds – gaudy, 'vulgar' plants – belong in this type of garden.
Camille Muller includes antique garden gnomes and a clothesline
with coloured pegs in his Parisian roof garden in homage to the
Alsatian grandmother who supplied many of his plants [*opposite*].[23]

At Le Clos du Pioule in the Ardèche (France)
Nicole Jalla-Cervlei grows over six hundred
varieties of flowers and vegetables on
narrow mountain terraces which she shares
with a retired mare, wild fauna of all shapes
and sizes, and her own sculptures, including
a particularly expressive wooden witch.

What objects are present, where do they come from, and what state are they in? Often preference is given to recycled things, obviously worn, with peeling paint – bedsteads turned into gates, coffee pots used for planters, and so on. For romantic souls, such choices evoke passing time, childhood memories, lost golden ages of intimacy with mother Earth (grandmothers), or sacred soil (*jardins de curé*). For practical grandmothers, recycling objects is both frugal and creative. Nicole Arboireau [*p. 56*] notes in Gabrielle's garden (one of those she describes in *Jardins de grands-mères*) a birdcage, a watering can, an old stove, a 1900 sewing machine, a coffee grinder, and a food mill painted teal blue.[24] Doudou Bayol, a grandmother gardening in Provence [*p. 59*], says simply: 'Make things yourself using whatever is at hand, that's the country way.' Today such an approach may also signify not only personal creativity but a rejection of consumer values.

A sophisticated urban designer, Camille Muller took inspiration from his Alsatian grandmother for his roof garden in Paris (France). Dense plantings blur scale and perspectives on many levels. He collected the antique garden gnomes, but she supplied cuttings and perhaps the colourful pegs on his clothesline.

LEFT AND OPPOSITE The artist Henk Gerritsen is also a learned naturalist, horticulturalist and successful author. In Priona, his garden in the Netherlands – his life's work – he shares his delight in playing with Nature. His creations, whether meadows, topiary, vegetable gardening, found sculpture or whimsical scarecrows, express the generous exuberance and enchanted partnership with all living creatures which characterize his approach to gardening.

What animals live in this garden? Country grandmothers often had a chicken coop or a rabbit hutch nearby. Where a garden is experienced daily, the gardener may enjoy nature's surprises rather than feel them as a threat. A pond or pool shelters frogs or draws dragonflies. The presence of bats and toads may mean unpolluted air and water. Ladybirds are obligatory, useful as well as delightful. Traditionally, cats are more at home here than dogs, perhaps because they are themselves intimate and sensual and love to explore small, hidden spaces in quiet ways. Birdfeeders are put on high branches or smooth poles. Fauna of all kinds contribute to the sounds of such a garden, rarely silent but usually serene. This is an Eden where the snake is an honoured guest.

Might you consider this an artist's garden? This style has greatly appealed to poets and painters – Rousseau, Wordsworth, Colette and Marcel Proust among them. Throughout the 19th century, minor genre paintings and engravings reinforced the sentimental version. Even Monet's Giverny [p. 147] might be linked to this genealogy. Anne Scott-James remarks that cottage gardening is not really a folk art. 'The idea of romantic simplicity, of usefulness wedded to charm, came from sophisticated people.'[25] But grandmothers' (and indeed sometimes grandfathers') gardens have always been created by people of all backgrounds. Many owners today practice an art or craft, sometimes mastered after retirement, and potters, makers of mosaics or objects from recycled iron, and so on, may proudly display their works in these gardens.

Anne-Marie Deloire, ceramic artist, invests her garden on the French Riviera with a multitude of colourful clay creations, crowding among the many plant varieties on several levels. She welcomes visitors and feels that their input is part of her creative process.

On the edge of the mountain village of Cordes-sur-Ciel, in south-western France, the designers Arnaud Maurières and Eric Ossart experimented with grandmotherly traditions of colour, texture, heirloom and annual plant associations, not forgetting the recyling of everyday objects. The Jardin des Paradis is now happily maintained by the township.

In this water feature at Cordes using ordinary galvanized buckets, Maurières and Ossart were inspired by a design made by Michel Desvignes and Christine Dalnoky at the International Garden Festival of Chaumont-sur-Loire (France) in 1993.

TWO VIEWS

Upon entering this so-called orchard, I was struck by a pleasantly cool sensation which dark shade, bright and lively greenery, flowers scattered on every side, the bubbling of flowing water, and the songs of a thousand birds impressed on my imagination at least as much as my senses ... I saw here and there without order or symmetry underbrush of rose, raspberry, and currant bushes, patches of lilac, hazel, elderberry, mock orange, broom, trifolium, which decked the earth while giving it a fallow appearance. I followed tortuous and irregular alleys bordered by those flowered woods, covered with a thousand garlands of Judean vine, creeper, hops, bindweed, bryony, clematis and other plants of that sort, among which honeysuckle and jasmine saw fit to mingle ...

Jean-Jacques Rousseau, *Julie, or the New Heloise*, 1761[26]

At first glance it is the overspilling plants which draw the eye. Clutter and confusion seem to rule. The garden is barely kept within its humble boundaries, and cannot resist the temptation to override them. It tumbles over the fence, climbs up into the neighbour's hedge, slips insidiously under the asphalt sidewalk.

This garden, unique and multifaceted, portrays its gardener.

Bright, big-blossomed roses delight the eye, herbs provide teas for all ailments, berry bushes supply fruit for jams, vegetables go into the indispensable evening soup, and many exotic plants, Mother's Day gifts from long ago, revert to their primal condition. Have no doubt, this gardener is at least seventy years old! Heedless of fashion, she has planted 'Staghorn' dahlias and sown Mexican zinnias ... This old garden has grown wild from too many successive passions, abandoned to the fierce struggle between plants, each one striving against its neighbour for a small patch of light and nourishing soil, and yet, this is a living garden, so very much alive!

Nicole Arboireau, *Jardins de grands-mères*, 1999[27]

The Jardin des Sambucs in the Gard (France) exemplifies today's country gardening on a shoestring, in small, often difficult spaces, owing its success to boundless enthusiasm and personal creativity. Its owners, Agnès and Nicolas Brückin, combine local tradition with global inspiration.

Ten Questions for Plantsmen's, Collectors', and Botanical Gardens

Have you ever noticed that botanical gardens often make you think of Paradise?
A zoo, no matter what, is more like Hell . . .

Francis Hallé, French botanist, 2004[28]

I am crazy about flowers and bamboos and I buy without counting, to the point of leaving
my family hungry for several days at a time or cold for a whole winter! I neglect the
needs of my mouth to satisfy my eye and ears. You may laugh at me but I am happy thus!

Chinese gardener Li Yu (1611–80), nicknamed 'Old Bamboo Hat of the Lake'[29]

What is the main goal or purpose of this collection? Scientific, conservationist, educational, aesthetic, all of the above? Scientific curiosity first motivated European plant collectors, plant hunters who combed the globe, often careless of their hunting grounds. Beginning in the 18th century, horticulturists seeking both beauty and rarity made many fine collections, some still extant. All these goals have had from their beginnings deep implications for the relationship between 'local' and 'global' forces in the world of plants and gardens. Most collectors have several motives at once: the authors of a guide to the botanical heritage of France count on a readership composed of 'lovers of gardens and rare plants, nurserymen and botanists looking for plants to multiply, and conservationists'.[30]

What is the history of this collection? Did it start with medicinal plants collected for a medieval university as in Padua or Montpellier? Was it built up in one place by successive generations, like the Parc Botanique de la Fosse in the Loire valley, begun in 1751? Did it emerge from the work of specialist nurseries painstakingly developing new varieties? Was it created as a major municipal park? As the result of a private passion, like Wigandia, in Australia [*p. 132*]? Collecting easily becomes obsessive: 'People for centuries have been fascinated by exotic plant material and the skills required to make it grow in unlikely conditions. They fuss over palm trees in greenhouses, in sheltered coves on the Irish and Scottish coasts, or in the lee of south-facing walls in southern Utah. Others breed and collect new species of plants.... The Roman emperor Hadrian collected souvenirs from all over his empire (which included most of the known world) at his villa at Tivoli, and sixteen centuries later the Chinese emperor Ch'ien Lung recalled, in a collection of gardens at the Yan Ming Yuan near Beijing, the varied splendours of his own enormous kingdom.'[31]

PREVIOUS PAGES
LEFT The Bambouseraie of Prafrance (France) began in 1856 with the fabulous exotic collections of plantsman Eugène Mazel. The Nègre family took possession in 1902 and made both its beautiful gardens of rare species and its bamboo nurseries world renowned. Muriel Nègre has today added a new dimension: site art.

RIGHT In 1898, the Bois des Moutiers gardens at Varengeville in Normandy (France) were first laid out with advice from Gertrude Jekyll around a house designed by Edwin Lutyens for the Mallet family, still in residence today. Its rhododendrons are particularly fine. Mallet descendants continue to be prominent plant collectors, notably of hydrangeas.

Lotusland at Santa Barbara, California (USA), once home to a 19th-century nurseryman, was transformed from 1941 by the Polish opera star Ganna Walska into gardens dramatically presenting cacti, euphorbias, aloes, bromeliads, succulents and cycads. But there are also orchards, topiary, ferns, Blue and Japanese gardens.

How are the collections organized? The criteria used may have evolved as the garden aged. In old-fashioned arboreta, trees were often lined up like regiments for close inspection, or like specimens in a museum, not always with concern for the best growing conditions and certainly not for aesthetic interest. Where beauty was also a goal, plants became parts of carefully composed pictures. Many old arboreta count among today's most beautiful gardens. Great botanical collections, often situated in city centres (Perth, New York, Cape Town, Singapore . . .), give pleasure even to those with no special scientific curiosity. Grouped plantings may illustrate common growing conditions, places of origin, species, or ethnobotanical features (uses made of the plants by humans). 'Plants are living beings, some shortlived, but many last for decades, even centuries, and create the framework of our own lives. They are part of our history, our culture; it is important to keep a record of their passing', writes the French botanist Brigitte Fourrier.[32]

The protected microclimate of Tresco Abbey Garden in the Isles of Scilly (UK) makes it possible to grow over 20,000 subtropical exotics outdoors, many from the southern hemisphere. The collections were started by Augustus Smith, an inspired philanthropist, in the 1830s and each successive generation of the Dorrien-Smith family has added more.

How do growing conditions in this garden compare with those of the plants' place of origin? In earlier times, a plant's original growing conditions were known only through the notes of plant hunters preparing albums of dried specimens now carefully preserved in major museums. Later, steamships made it easier to transport living plants, so that eager collectors could experiment with acclimatizing treasures from far away. Today, there are parks that re-create whole ecosystems to welcome plants from other continents. Both the Strybing Arboretum in San Francisco and the Domaine du Rayol in France imitate Mediterranean plant communities from five continents. Sometimes plants are assembled that need similar growing conditions (the same 'biome'), although brought from far-flung corners of the earth. At the Filippi nursery gardens in southern France [p. 164], drought tolerance is evaluated in specimens from Australia, Malta, South Africa . . .[33]

Inverewe Garden, on the west coast of the Scottish Highlands, begun in 1862 by Osgood Mackenzie, is protected from extreme temperatures by warm currents from the Caribbean. Managed today by the National Trust for Scotland, it houses national collections of *Brachyglottis, Olearia, Ourisisia* and *Rhododendron* (*barbata* subsection).

Do the organizers of these collections take a stand in the ongoing quarrel about native and exotic plants? The speed and volume of species intermingling worldwide has greatly increased in recent decades. Are exotic 'vagabonds' inevitably 'invasive' and destructive of local varieties? When growing conditions change due to building or pollution, 'natives' can also spread unpredictably. Will long-term effects offset short-term disruption of natural habitats or will species loss be irreversible? Native plant supporters in North America, South Africa and Australia strive to keep out 'aliens' to minimize risks. In Europe however the situation is different. A scientific survey in Sheffield claims that 'few British natives are garden worthy and thus virtually all the ornamental plants seen in British gardens are exotics'.[34] Home gardeners sometimes affect local ecosystems unknowingly by introducing plants which spread. Might that be an issue in this garden?

Kirstenbosch, South Africa's National Botanical Garden, near Cape Town, is much admired both for its magnificent collections and for its setting. Founded in 1913, the estate of 528 hectares (some 1,300 acres) includes *fynbos*, natural forest and cultivated garden. Only indigenous South African plants are grown here.

At their imaginative Sorrento Gardens near Melbourne in Australia, professional designer Fiona Brockhoff and her partner David Swann have used native plants that blend seamlessly with the coastal setting. They concentrate on varieties that require little water and feeding and attract native fauna.

Do the species represented also have their own history, stories, symbols, myths? Often owners or managers of collections provide documents, answer questions or themselves tell stories about their most famous specimens. Most botanical gardens are carefully labelled. The link between botany and travel provides many fascinating stories. In France in 1690, at the fortress of Rochefort, a monk named Charles Plumier brought back from South America six little plants to which the *intendant*, Michel Bégon, gave his name: the begonia. Today the fortress boasts 'Homecoming Gardens' designed by Bernard Lassus in homage to plant hunters. The Brazilian collector and pioneer ecologist Roberto Burle Marx, travelling as a young man in Europe, found that South American species were much prized in Frankfurt but completely neglected, in his day, at home. He went on to collect more than three thousand native tropical species in his gardens, Sítio Santo Antonio da Bica in Campo Grande [*pp. 126–27, 188*].

What role does fauna play in this garden? Are these gardens maintained using chemicals that are dangerous to other forms of life? Is there an attempt to establish a balance between flora, fauna and even bacteria, perhaps, through the use of compost, manure, mulches, etc.? Can one re-create an exotic ecosystem without fauna? Are there examples of co-evolution or interdependency between the plants and the fauna that live among them? Sir Thomas Hanbury, when he first imported yuccas into his Italian garden [p. 80], only gradually realized that he would also need to import an essential companion insect to pollinate the flowers. Subtropical and tropical botanical gardens consider brilliantly coloured birds the inevitable complement to floral display. As a rule, the presence of fauna adds movement and counteracts any museum-like mood in plant collections.

Is there a definite itinerary for walking around this garden, and if so, how was this determined? Many collectors' gardens were laid out originally to allow full inspection of specimens by visitors. A guided visit to the Marnier-Lapostolle Garden on the Riviera, the largest private botanical collection in the world, leads first through a vast park, then through each of twenty-two greenhouses. Even in public botanical gardens where visitors usually wander at will, map in hand, there is far too much to absorb in a single visit. Many famous collections organize whole areas as showcases for particular species. Even in a relatively small home garden this can be done: at the Agapanthe Gardens in Normandy [p. 84] (originally 1,500 square metres, now 6,000) there is a redwood walk, a 'kalapanax' terrace, a wild garden, collections of agapanthus, hostas and veronicas, sedum and daphnes, a euphorbia amphitheatre, a series of ponds . . .

The Jardin Plume in Normandy (France), created by Patrick and Sylvie Quibel in 2002, proves that plant collecting, ecological awareness and strong contemporary design are not incompatible. Like many collectors, the Quibels also run a nursery of choice perennials and grasses.

LEFT In 1867, the English philanthropist Sir Thomas Hanbury, returning from China, purchased La Mortola on the Italian Riviera for experiments in acclimatizing exotics. He first saw this steep hillside from a rowboat at sea. Access is still limited to the road at the very top, the sea, or the ancient Roman Via Aurelia which runs through the gardens.

BELOW The Huntington Botanical Gardens, at San Marino in California (USA), form part of an estate that also houses fine art and rare book collections. Organized by theme, the plantings include desert gardens (here American agaves), Japanese, Chinese and Australian gardens, a rose garden, a jungle garden, and much more.

OPPOSITE The French plantsman Patrick Blanc now designs vertical gardens on city buildings all over the world – in Paris, for the new anthropological Musée des Arts Premiers, seen here, and the Pershing Hotel. But Blanc is also a highly respected botanist, veteran of many expeditions to remote tropical forests.

How do the collections relate to their setting? Can you examine specimens from all sides? Is some individual treasure dramatically framed? Is there a layered arrangement or a sequence of green rooms? If there is a greenhouse, are plants visible at several different heights or distances? In park-like settings, are species presented as a series of episodes? Are you allowed to leave the path to examine them closely, walk all around them, read labels close up? Are they presented artfully? The most spectacular union between rare plants and an architectural setting today is achieved in the vertical or wall gardens made famous by Patrick Blanc [*above*], who has now created versions of his invention from California to Australia. His plant communities are designed to evolve with a life of their own. Himself a modern-day plant hunter, he also plans with an artist's eye.

Are these collections connected to a public institution, an association, a famous plant fair, a teaching organization? Are they part of a garden network with sites elsewhere you might like to visit? Many of the best garden varieties sold today have awards of merit from the Royal Horticultural Society, the American Horticultural Association, or prestigious plant fairs such as Courson near Paris. Most Western countries have comparable awards, and most now have protected national collections for different plant species situated in parks and gardens all over the territory. If you enjoyed your first visit, it should be easy to get further information and even take a study course, if you wish. The most famous collections – at Kew Gardens near London [*below*], the Jardin des Plantes in Paris, Mainau in Germany, and Dumbarton Oaks in the US, to name just a few, offer extensive educational programmes for people of all ages and backgrounds.

Famous since the 1600s, the Royal Botanic Gardens at Kew (near London, UK) boast collections enriched by royal patrons, intrepid plant hunters and gifted directors. As a result, this institution is today one of the world's most important centres for research and education. The great Palm House was built in 1845, a pioneering work of iron architecture.

ABOVE The Château de Courson (south-west of Paris, France) holds twice-yearly plant fairs that attract specialists from throughout the world. But the beautiful gardens of this distinguished château, including this pond created in 1860 by the distinguished Bühler brothers, contain many fine specimens and are well worth a visit throughout the year.

TWO VIEWS

I am going to tell you how to recognize a true gardener. 'You must come and see me,' he says, 'I want to show you my garden.' When you go, thinking to please him, you find yourself addressing his posterior as he bends down among his plants. 'I'll just be a moment,' he says, looking up over his arm, 'just take a minute to plant this.' 'Please,' you insist courteously, 'do not go to any trouble.' After some time he has no doubt finished; in any case, he rises, dirties your hand, and speaks, his face radiantly hospitable: 'Do come and see: it's just a little garden, of course, but ... oh, just a minute ...' He bends down to pull up a few weeds from a flower bed. 'Come along then, I'm going to show you a *Dianthus musalae*, you have never seen anything like it! Oh dear, there's a bit I forgot to dig !' And he stops to poke at the soil. After a quarter of an hour he stands up straight again and says, 'oh yes, I wanted to show you those bluebells, that's a *Campanula wilsonae*. The most beautiful variety, one that ... oh wait, I must tie up that delphinium.' When this has been done, he stops to think: 'You surely want to see my *erodium*. We'll just get to it after I move that aster, it's a little to close to its neighbour.' At this point, you tiptoe away, leaving behind his posterior, as he bends down to his plants ...

Karel Capek, *The Gardener's Year*, 1929[35]

A 'remediation' planting in Australia, on Botany Bay: Bruce Mackenzie recreated what he assumed was the original dune configuration, manipulating the topography with precision. Amongst this he planted indigenous species. The assumption was that they would simply regenerate themselves once they were taken 'home' ... Twenty years later, the planting was reaching its end, and weeds rather than the indigenous species were regenerating ... It was ironic that the plants brought over to Australia for gardeners now do better than the plants that were here originally, and that the efforts of gardening now must be used to maintain the native plants.

    ... Europe is a cosmopolitan place, a place where people and organisms had been moving for thousands of years. This seemed to lead to an attitude where growth itself, rather than a biologically arbitrary classification such as native/non-native, was valued as the central property of vegetation. I have now realised that humans can impose an ideology on nature, but it won't respond with one. Its logic is strictly pragmatic and ecological.

Julian Raxworthy, Australian landscape architect, 2006[36]

The Agapanthe Gardens in Normandy
(France), created by Alexandre Thomas from
1996, prove that impressive botanical variety
can be displayed even in a small-scale setting.

Ten Questions for Kitchen Gardens, Cooks' Gardens, and Potagers

All continents live in my garden. The strangest flavours, tastes, and shapes are all accommodated here. The graceful claytonia from Cuba keeps company with the spiny golden thistle (Scolymus) from Spain, while the Jerusalem artichoke converses with the Japanese knotroot (Stachys affinis).

Jean-Luc Danneyrolles, *Le Jardin extraordinaire*, 2001

I want death to find me planting my cabbages, indifferent to his coming and even more so to the imperfect state of my garden.

Michel de Montaigne, 1580[37]

Why are vegetables grown in this garden? Is it a farm, family, weekend or cook's garden? If so, how many does it feed and how often? Perhaps it is mainly ornamental, laid out for private or public pleasure (a designer creation, the potager of a château or other historic monument?). Is it charming by accident or design? Does it have a teaching vocation (as part of an ecomuseum or organic gardening training centre)? Is it managed in aid of the long-term unemployed or recent immigrants, just as the first allotments once helped factory workers during the Industrial Revolution? Is it proudly displayed near the house for easy access, or set apart, as in French châteaux or English 'landscape' parks, as vulgarly utilitarian? Some of those walled château potagers, once thought unworthy, now redone by top designers, have become major tourist destinations, as at Miromesnil, Galleville and Bosmelet in Normandy.

PREVIOUS PAGES
Four generations transformed Le Cerf restaurant at Marlenheim in Alsace (France) from a country inn to a gastronomic mecca. Robert Husser's vegetable garden was a gift from a grateful couple of market gardeners whom he fed daily, for free, when they were too old to work. Today Robert and his son collaborate in the kitchen and Robert still grows herbs and salads, often carried to the kitchen by the youngest in the line …

The Château de Saint-Jean-de-Beauregard, near Paris in France, holds two plant fairs a year: for perennials in April and vegetables in November. Its owners, the Curels, with help from the designer Eric Ossart, created a freer mix of vegetables, herbs, fruit and flowers more in tune with today's tastes than the old, strict formality.

French allotment gardens – here at Ivry, near Paris – were first laid out by late 19th-century industrialists wanting to keep their factory workers safe from the demon drink. In those days women were not admitted, but today allotments have become true family gardens.

Who does the actual digging? Owners or employees? Men or women? French farm gardens were tended by women, while working-class allotments were exclusively male until very recently. Who follows the weather patterns daily, monthly and yearly in this garden? Vegetable gardening may be the only kind where back-breaking jobs are undertaken with real enthusiasm: 'To lift and penetrate and tear apart the soil is a labour – a pleasure – always accompanied by an exaltation that no unprofitable exercise can ever provide', wrote Colette.[38] Another French writer, Henri Cueco, asked his gardener, 'When is a garden good, in your experience?' The gardener replied: 'When the vegetables are happy, when it's neat, when it thanks me for my good work.'[39] Vegetable gardeners all over the world – owners or hired help, men or women – often take great pride in their efforts and like to show off, and share, their production.

How are the beds laid out, and where are they seen from? Do you discover this garden along a country road or from a nearby hill? If visitors are allowed, can you see everything from the gate or the terrace above, as at the famous Château de Villandry [*p. 52*] (one of Rosemary Verey's inspirations at Barnsley House in England [*opposite*])? Is the layout determined by existing topography and site contours? Are walls also put to good use? Are the beds flat or on a slope? Do they have harmonious proportions? La Quintinie, vegetable gardener at Versailles in the 17th century, wrote: 'The best figure for a Fruit or Kitchen Garden and most convenient for Culture is a beautiful Square of straight angles, being once and a half if not twice as long as it is broad.'[40] Is there easy access to the beds from the paths? Does their outline remain clear or soon get smothered in overspilling vegetation? Are they edged with stones or tiles or flowers (the classic marigolds) or evergreen borders (box? lavender?)? Their width is a clue to what equipment is used and also to how many visitors are expected.

Ballymaloe Cookery School Gardens, near Cork in Ireland, are the creation of chef Darina Allen, combining beauty and productivity. Their formal beds are most impressive seen from a slightly higher level. The restaurant and school have their own 100-acre (40-hectare) organically run farm.

The gardens of Barnsley House in Gloucestershire (England), laid out from 1951 by Rosemary Verey in the Arts and Crafts style so long influential in British gardening. Verey's ornamental potager became an icon, itself inspired by the formal vegetable parterres of the Château de Villandry in France.

What methods and materials are commonly used here? Is there one consistent approach – biodynamic, organic, intensive, extensive, careless, compulsive, etc.? Are 'hard' chemicals deemed unavoidable, either as fertilizers or pesticides, or is management purely organic? Are the crops mulched with straw, grass clippings or any other material? Are some spaces sown with green manure crops (clovers, phacelia, etc.)? Is self-sowing tolerated? Encouraged? Is this the intensive gardening on small raised beds that William Robinson admired in Paris already in the 1860s, 'these little family gardens as they may be called, usually no longer than admits of the owner's eye telling the condition of every crop in the garden all at once'.[41] Where does the water come from, and how is it distributed? Is some wild fauna welcomed, perhaps with a pond? What material is used to lay out paths – temporary (boards) or permanent (paved)? Are there places to sit down? Are constructions store-bought, homemade according to a plan, or assembled with recycled materials in a seemingly haphazard manner?

How are the plants chosen and associated? Are the vegetables
current and common varieties, regional, heirloom, hybrid,
genetically modified? What methods are used to make new
plants? Are seeds, cuttings and transplants produced on the spot?
If so, is there a greenhouse? Are the vegetables planted in careful
rows, or with the crazy patterns produced by finding last-minute
space for a new crop? Are vegetables mixed with flowers, herbs,
small fruit and fruit trees, either espaliered or full size? Nostalgia
for medieval gardens often inspires ornamental potagers today
because medieval documents list, for example, roses and lilies
as medicinal plants, thereby authorizing a happy intermingling.
Whatever the history, pleasure, beauty and productivity blend
unabashedly in kitchen gardens today. Organic gardeners also mix
flowers, herbs, vegetables and fruit to benefit from the effects of
'companion' planting: tomatoes like carrots and each improves
the other's growth and flavour.

Alix de Saint Venant, owner of the Château
de Valmer wine domain in the Loire valley
(France), developed its beautiful potager
as a conservatory for over three thousand
vegetable varieties, to help fight draconian
European seed restrictions. Every August,
Valmer features these gourds at its lively
Festival of Saint Fiacre.

What appeals here to the eye, the nose, the touch, the palate?
Does this garden have long, formally balanced perspectives, as in many historic château gardens? Or impressionist clouds of soft colour (as at Saint-Jean-de-Beauregard near Paris [*p.* 88], for example)? Bright, warm and mixed colours are often appreciated in kitchen gardens – the reds and oranges of squash, pumpkin, peppers. When looks count most, cropping is done all at once so as not to make holes in neat rows. In the famous formal gardens at Villandry [*p.* 52], for example, everything is removed and replaced twice in each growing season. In more intimate gardens, touch and smell play a larger part. Many fragrant plants – tansy, wormwood, lavender – are grown to protect vegetables from pests, either by simple proximity or in home-made spray preparations. As for flavour – will you have a chance to taste?

Bingerden Gardens, in the province of Gelderland in the Netherlands, owned by the same family since 1660, hold their celebrated plant fair every year in June. This walled potager once covered 2 acres (just under 1 hectare) – the traditional size for châteaux) – but now, reduced by half, lays out its vegetable rows against orchards and floral borders.

Who cooks and eats this produce? Are the vegetables served up for family dinners, community meals, at a bed-and-breakfast supper table, in a great restaurant? Most chefs working with kitchen gardens or experimental farms make up their menus according to the day's produce, like Dan Barber at Stone Barns near New York [*below*]. At the Prieuré d'Orsan in central France [*p. 15*], where almost everything grown is edible, the owner-cook Patrice Taravella uses what he can and sells the rest to visitors as preserves. Many cooks keep a garden simply to help educate customers who have never seen, for example, an artichoke bud ready to harvest. In the USA, the fashion for vegetable gardening grew apace with interest in American cuisine, thanks largely to the pioneer Alice Waters in Berkeley in the 1970s. Waters also labours to educate the young, promoting vegetable gardening in school yards.

BELOW Stone Barns, near New York (USA), combines a working farm, educational centre facilities and a restaurant, Blue Hill, run by the Barber family (chef Dan Barber). The centre's mission is to 'celebrate, teach and advance community-based food production and enjoyment, from farm to classroom to table'.

OPPOSITE Chef Raymond Blanc's vegetable and herb garden at the Manoir aux Quat' Saisons in Oxfordshire (England) produces over 90 types of vegetables and 70 types of herb in its 2 acres (just under 1 hectare), to supply the kitchen of the restaurant with its daily needs for eight months of the year.

How does this garden look throughout the year, from season to season?
Vegetable gardens more than any other change from hour to hour, day to day, month to month. Each season involves work to prepare the next which is bound to look completely different. Owners who receive the public take full advantage of this evolution to organize seasonal events and festivities. The Château de Valmer in the Loire valley [p. 92] is a prime example, with events season-long, culminating in the Festival de Saint Fiacre every August. Visitors rarely visit public properties at night, but home gardeners know that moonlight among the vegetables can be magic, and many of the garden's secret inhabitants are active then. In winter, only other vegetable growers will be interested, perhaps, though gardeners experiment with beautiful wrappings for half-hardy perennials like cardoons. Vegetable gardening, the most seasonal of all, helps people savour each moment of the day and of the year.

Heronswood Gardens near Melbourne, Australia, show visitors three different vegetable gardens, two perennial gardens ('hot' and 'pastel'), plus subtropical and landscaped fruit gardens. There is also a nursery supplying over 800 varieties of 'Digger's seeds and plants' and a thatched-roofed café.

Does this garden leave scope for play and whimsy? A place of colourful and ever-changing display invites playful experimentation, whether in outline, theme or colour combinations. In France this produces the leaf-shaped potager at La Châtonnière or the artistic orchards of Drulon (both in the Loire region) or the Rainbow Gardens at Bosmelet (Normandy). When the potager is just one in a series of theme gardens, it is often the public's favourite, especially with children. Potagers were the theme chosen for the International Garden Festival at Chaumont in 1999, a season still well remembered. The agronomist Olivier de Serres, one of the first to discover new vegetables arriving from the Americas, was mainly concerned with helping rural populations survive; but he did not separate subsistence from pleasure when he wrote in 1600, 'These are pottages which furnish useful ornament to our household, countless types of root, herb, flower and fruit, with many marvels.'[42]

The Laquenexy Orchard in Lorraine, France (part of the Gardens Without Limits network linking France, Germany and Luxembourg), was the brainchild of garden designer Pascal Garbe. It combines education and entertainment in fourteen themed spaces mixing vegetables, flowers, herbs and fruit.

Is this kitchen garden linked to an agrarian or utopian ideal?

Food gardening, a universal human activity, is an essential part of any model community. Many movements and foundations today link food for the world to social cohesion and spiritual well-being, such as Slow Food (based in Italy), or research centres such as the Terre Vivante (Living Earth) centre in the Alps [*below*], the Amanins Centre of the agronomist Pierre Rabhi in northern Provence, or Garden Organic in Britain [*opposite*]. Many food-producing utopias, both public and private, have been influenced by visionaries like Rudolf Steiner. Lanzo del Vasto urged people to 'Find the shortest way between the earth, the hands and the mouth'[43] – advice which, quoted on Dan Barber's website at the Stone Barns model farm near New York [*p. 94*], is ever more relevant today. Is the garden you are visiting in this sense a community effort? One you might share by taking a course or reading some of their publications?

OPPOSITE Garden Organic (formerly the Henry Doubleday Research Association), at Ryton in Warwickshire, is Britain's leading organic growing charity, at the forefront of this horticulture movement for fifty years, dedicated more than ever to researching and promoting this approach to gardening, farming and food.

RIGHT In France, a committed group of ecologists founded first a magazine and a publishing house, then the Terre Vivante experimental and educational centre in the Alps. Symbolic 'Gardens of the Elements' were laid out around the farmhouse ruins by the leading French ecologist Gilles Clément.

TWO VIEWS

Finding the best food and doing things the simplest way sometimes feels complicated, but there is nothing very mysterious about it, nor is it something only restaurants can do. You only need to open your eyes – and all your other senses . . . within a short time after we opened, an assortment of people began to show up at our kitchen door, drawn by our reputation for culinary curiosity. Neighbors began bringing us bunches of radishes, sorrel, and herbs from their backyard gardens – for free or in trade . . . Good food depends almost entirely on good ingredients.

Alice Waters, restaurant cook in Berkeley, California, in *Chez Panisse Vegetables*, 1996

The productive home garden provides the best model for managing the world. It has proven its worth for centuries. If we add today what we know about the life of the soil and of plants, and make equitable use of modern technologies, we should be able to establish a durable and optimal harmony with the Earth.

Pierre Lieutaghi, French ethnobotanist, in *Le Sauvage*, 1980

At West Green House Gardens in Hampshire (England) the Australian designer Marilyn Abbott mixes globes of weigelia and viburnum with her rows of vegetables in an exuberant and imaginative contemporary interpretation of older formal styles.

Ten Questions for Outdoor Art

Sculpture? . . . a fashionable whim or a real temptation to have something beautiful in your garden? . . . In fact, it is rather our times which are out of joint with all our talk of flowers, or nature without human beings. For two thousand years, sculpture has belonged in gardens.

Danielle Dagenais, garden columnist for the Montreal daily newspaper *Le Devoir*, 1995[44]

As an artist, Noguchi faced a classic dilemma: that of the sculptor who tries to create an object in space with sufficient intrinsic energy to command that space – yet also yearns to make the space itself energetic and memorable.

Peter Walker and Melanie Simo, *Invisible Gardens*, 1992[45]

Does the art stand out from its setting? In traditional sculpture parks, works are distinguished from a neutral green background by their colours, shapes and materials. It is the artworks which are labelled, not the plants, whose function is to provide discreet enhancement for the main focus. The art is produced elsewhere, then brought and placed on site. If the works were intended to be merely decorative or atmospheric, they may not however have much value on their own. (Sculpture in private gardens has been called 'the rich man's garden gnome'!) The Californian artist and gardener Martha Kingsbury offers this guide: 'It is art if it is good enough to seem really excellent and "like art" in a lot of other environments besides where you are seeing it. And, it is also art, of a different and situated sort, if it is so effective and right in its place that nothing else would do there and any change would feel like a sort of violence to both it and the place.'

An urn on a hill at the Château de Marqueyssac (Dordogne, France) may suggest art dominating nature; but in fact, this elegant restoration of a dramatic site insists rather on fruitful dialogue between human inhabitants, other species and local landscapes.

PREVIOUS PAGES
LEFT At the César Manrique Foundation in the Canary Islands (Spain), the black volcanic rock of a former quarry combines with architectural cactus collections and the organic forms of the artist's own creations to express a personal vision of art in nature.

RIGHT At the Norton Simon Museum in Pasadena, California (USA), important collections of contemporary art are housed in a building recently renovated by Frank Gehry Associates, and extended outdoors into imaginative sculpture gardens created by Nancy Goslee Power.

Does the art dramatically change your perception of setting as a whole? The American poet Wallace Stevens imagined a simple jar so well placed upon a hill that 'The wilderness rose up to it, /And sprawled around, no longer wild.'[46] This image influenced generations of landscape architects for whom an artefact – sculpture or building – could transform 'raw' nature into art. In this case, the designer's art consists of choosing and placing the right object. As a result of this act, nature becomes subject to art (the jar 'took dominion everywhere'). The minimalist landscape architect Peter Walker deems that 'the dependence on objects to command space is still perhaps the supreme strategy of modern Western design'. But he commends the sculptor Isamu Noguchi for his achievement in escaping this 'dependence on the object, singular or composed, as focus'.[47] In the Japanese-American's work [*pp. 178–79*], Walker admired 'the sense of place as significant space rather than as mere setting'. Do single objects stand out here as focal points, pulling the picture together, or are all elements equally important, the relations between objects as much as the objects themselves?

Ian Hamilton Finlay's seminal works at Little Sparta in southern Scotland often involve the written word, allowing visitors to experience his garden as 'a metaphor for Western culture'. Poetry, sculpted stone and setting all interact, no single focus dominating the others.

Are elements of the place directly involved in the fabric of the artworks? Could the works have been made anywhere else? The garden historian Tim Richardson concurs with Walker: 'Conceptualist landscape designers are not creating stand-alone art objects which might also be imaginable in a gallery space or sculpture garden; they are making spaces which will be used by people and which will change and develop over time.'[48] Which and how much of the materials used to create the work(s) of art are taken from the place itself? Today, artists working directly on site integrate foliage, rocks, wood, water, and even weather patterns into their creations. Sometimes the landscape itself is sculpted and formed, as with century-old hillside terracing. Such creations are said to be site-generated or site-determined. The term 'land art', once used for a different American movement in the 1970s, has been revived for this new direction, also called 'earth' or 'nature' art.

BELOW For his private garden in the south of France, nurseryman Jean-Marie Rey chose works by the Riviera artist Sacha Sosno representing figures from Greek mythology – Venus de Milo on the left and Apollo on the right. These were placed by the owner, not made for the site.

OPPOSITE At the Hannah Peschar outdoor sculpture gallery in Surrey (England), 'stand-alone art objects' are set in and framed by managed landscape, to be viewed from predetermined vantage points and distance. They are replaced by others when sold.

***From what vantage point(s), what height or depth, what angles
or positions do you encounter the work(s)?*** To admire English
mixed borders or Japanese Zen gardens, you stand in front of
them, as you would look at pictures in a gallery. At the Ton ter
Linden gardens in Holland, a raised platform even imposes a
specific angle of vision and distance from the beautiful floral
arrangements below. At the Hannah Peschar outdoor sculpture
gallery in Surrey [*p. 107*], you move through a landscape to discover
tastefully composed scenes made of artworks, water and plants,
balanced with a photographer's eye for distance and framing.
Offered for sale and often changed, the sculptures are viewed from
specific, determined vantage points along set paths. Parks like
Villaret [*p. 113*] and Vassivière in France let visitors touch and play
with works built on site and inseparable from it. An extreme
variant is practised by George Hargreaves (American) and Jacques
Simon (French), who both create land or field art to be seen from
an aeroplane! Treetop walks in Australia, Singapore and Florida
allow visitors to explore managed landscapes from above.

Isabelle Greene at the much photographed
Valentine Garden in California (USA) lets
her terraced plantings echo vast landscapes
seen from an aeroplane, with rivers and
lakes, a disconcerting play with expectations
of scale that needs a viewpoint from above.

The French land artist Erik Samakh constructed this 'Waterwork' (*Pièce d'eau*) for the gardens of the Château de Barbirey in Burgundy in 1997. Its elegant bamboo structure protected frog populations reintroduced by the artist, whose work often involves sound as well as sight.

How does scale matter here, in connection to the site, the work and yourself? Angle of vision may imply differences of scale which can be used to enhance contact, discovery, enjoyment. Are you walking eight miles – some twelve kilometres – to discover, for example, Goldsworthy's 'Art Refuges' in Provence? Or do you need to 'look twice' to see the painted tree trunk at the Albarède Gardens in the Dordogne, where a small gesture has transformed nature into art? Is the scale of the site comfortable, human, with pictures already composed, or is there a challenging and delightful confusion between big and small? In 1995, at the Château de Barbirey in Burgundy, Bernard Lassus made ink drawings on château windows superimposed on garden views outside, creating a dialogue between historic and current, imaginary and real, small and life-size versions, in which each visitor mixed a personal cocktail.[49]

ABOVE The British artist Andy Goldsworthy plays with time, from geological eons to the instant impact of snow and rain. His solid stone cairns in Provence (France) follow hidden streams and echo mountain shapes, in art which is completely 'site-generated' and integrated.

OPPOSITE Festivals combine gardening and contemporary art on a temporary basis. In 2002, at Chaumont (France), three designers from the Beth Galí agency in Barcelona, together with the artist Luís Bisbe and the gardener Alex Aquilar, invited visitors to peep through veils in this 'Soft-focus Garden' (*Jardin flou*). That year's theme was eroticism.

Are you invited or expected to participate actively in some way?

Andy Goldsworthy designed his 'Art Refuges' for hikers, so that they might 'sleep and wake up to a sculpture', thus establishing 'a more intimate relationship between the viewer and the work. It is the difference between living with and looking at – an observer or a participant.'[50] The contemporary art philosopher Anne Cauquelin reflects on garden festivals where, she feels, the visitors 'by their way of walking round inside a work determine its meaning and the story it tells. Spectators become active participants, not only actors, but co-authors.'[51] Today artists often invite closer contact, mixing inside and out, architecture, sculpture and garden. Traditional features like pergolas, sheltered walkways and 'green rooms' play new roles, where transitions count as much as the spaces linked. You may be encouraged to look up or down, to sit, climb, kneel or even to lie down, in order to make meaningful contact with the work. At the very least, to walk around and through it.

What role is given to living, growing elements in this work?

American Land Art of the 1970s concentrated on entropy, destruction, dissolution, death. Gardeners by definition promote growth. Decomposition for them means compost – the potential of new life. Today, according to Anne Cauquelin, contemporary artists are tempted 'to change mediums and, since they like to work with process, to experiment with plants, with living materials'.[52] The Australian landscape architect Julian Raxworthy admires the Valle de Hebron in Spain, designed by Eduard Bru, where the architecture 'has been able to engage the natural processes in the site and those processes are now producing new forms'.[53] Christine Picasso describes the tree pruner Marc Nucera in Provence as a 'sculptor of living plants'.[54] His 'sculptural pruning' is the contrary of bonsais or topiary, since it links the tree to its chosen site and allows for its future development. Today the term 'land art' is used for works that include growth as well as decay.

Living sculpture has traditionally meant topiary, but today's designers, while still depending on broadleaf evergreens, work more as architects. In this private garden, Jacques Wirtz and Sons brilliantly redefine a site with sculpted hedges, pleached trees, walls and water.

Is this outdoor art instantaneous, transitory, or durable through time? Classical sculpture was inspired by and intended for eternity. Much contemporary art, said the American philosopher Susan Sontag, 'is produced not by pregnancy and childbirth but by a blind date'.[55] Outdoors, the date may be with the weather or the summer visitor; the work may be a rain shadow lasting moments, or festival installations visible for only a season. Is this a conflict or a convergence between gardens and outdoor art? Gardens have always given pleasure on a whole range of time scales, incorporating the moment as well as centuries. Robert Irwin had – permanently – carved into the plaza floor of the Central Garden at the Getty Foundation in Los Angeles the words: 'Always changing, never twice the same'. Very near this inscription, gardeners working at night remove half the foliage of plane trees to maintain the artist's desired balance of light and shade. Change and control are two poles in any garden.

At the remote Vallon du Villaret (Lozère, France), visitors zigzag back and forth across a trout stream, encountering works of art constructed especially for the site. These can be walked through, rolled in, smelt, touched, listened to – almost everything but eaten.

What senses are engaged by this work besides sight? If you climb over it or sleep inside it, you will be responding with more than your eyes! The British designer Dan Pearson [*p. 121*] judges that all gardens 'sharpen the senses'. Today many artists include both sound and scent in outdoor art. Both are pervasive: you can close your eyes but less easily your ears or your nose. The sounds of water, birds and wind chimes are traditional, of course.[56] But gardens today, long in thrall to the eyes alone, are appealing more and more to other senses, thanks in part to the experiment of artists working outdoors. Bernard Lassus taught generations of French students that landscape is 'a balanced interaction between touch, sound, smell and sight'.[57] Alexandre Chemetoff's celebrated bamboo gardens at the Parc de La Villette in Paris include an effective sound cylinder by Bernhard Leitner.

What relationship does the art imply between humankind and nature? If the art no longer 'takes dominion everywhere' like Wallace Stevens's jar, then what alternative attitudes towards nature may it express? The British earth artist Richard Long, famous for stone lines and walking art, wrote in 1991 that he explored places 'where my human characteristics meet the natural forces and patterns of the world, and that is really the subject of my work'.[58] Today, many place makers query the West's traditional split between nature and culture, rejecting both domination and submission (the Romantic mode). Both stances imply human separation from the biosphere, whereas many today propose participation, even celebration, a humanist ecology.[59] The dialogue between human creation and 'natural' settings (themselves often already the result of human intervention) recalls what the modernist Christopher Tunnard, encouraging non-representational sculpture in gardens, named 'empathy'.[60]

The Bibémus quarries near Aix-en-Provence (France) were a favourite subject of the painter Paul Cézanne. In 2006, they were sensitively restored by Philippe Deliau and Hélène Bensoam of ALEP to communicate site memory, edit views and preserve ecosystems. The result is a fine new work of nature art.

TWO VIEWS

There is a difference between placing and making a work on a site. A work made in a place grows there and becomes part of it in a way that a sited object has difficulty in achieving ... At times it is difficult to say where my touch ends and the place begins. This lack of division can at times be disturbing. It is easier and in some ways more pleasing to make a sculpture work through its contrast to the surroundings, but the greater challenge is to make work that is completely welded to its site.

Andy Goldsworthy *Time*, 2002[61]

Sculpture : a limited object, awkward, sublime by the directions it reveals. For that to happen there must be a space, a lighted stage. We look at that white house over there and think it could not be more ordinary. A cloud passes on the horizon, it will suddenly be illuminated from afar. This will be only a momentary flash ...

Gilles Clément, 'Art depends on the Cooking' (a defence of 'involuntary art'), 2006[62]

Brigitte Lapouge-Déjean, an organic gardening writer, and Serge Lapouge, a sculptor-designer, have together created the Albarède Gardens in the Dordogne (France). Their soft meadows, kitchen garden and wild box sculpted for seasonal display are proof that land art can be done at home with limited material investment.

Ten Questions for Natural, Naturalistic, and Wild Gardens

*We should compose from Nature, as landscape artists do. We may have in our gardens –
and without making wildernesses of them – all the shade, the relief, the grace, the beauty,
and nearly all the irregularity of Nature.*

William Robinson, *The Parks and Gardens of Paris*, 1878[63]

*The garden . . . real terrain, mysterious but explorable, it invites the gardener – Man –
to define its space, its wealth, its habitat. It holds humanity suspended in time. Each seed
announces tomorrow. It is always a project. The garden produces goods, bears symbols,
accompanies dreams. It is accessible to everyone. It promises nothing and gives everything.*

Gilles Clément, *Une Ecologie humaniste*, 2006[64]

Are 'natural' effects here spontaneous or contrived to look that way?

Does water, for example, flow of its own accord or as the result of complex engineering? In the 18th century landscape parks obtained a spontaneous look by dint of great effort and expense behind the scenes.[65] In the 1930s, Dutch gardeners created beautiful islands of artificial wilderness in their famous Heemparks. The British biologist Nigel Dunnett admits that current 'naturalistic' gardens are 'highly managed, artificial interpretations of nature' but claims that, because of their ecological sensitivity, they 'seem far more meaningful and satisfying than gardens produced for ornament alone'.[66] Other gardeners work directly with living ecosystems, participating with minimum control or direction. In extreme cases, the 'garden' may simply be a naturalist's observation ground. Can you make out how much human intervention has contributed to the 'natural' effects of this garden, and what forms it took? Are the practical underpinnings cleverly hidden?

At Denmans Garden in Sussex (England), John Brookes has long experimented with a 'glorious disarray', artful but unforced. A pioneer designer and writer, he early on linked gardening both to international art trends and to ecology, insisting on respect for local character and settings.

PREVIOUS PAGES

LEFT Piet Oudolf's 'naturalistic' plantings at the Pensthorpe Millennium Gardens and Wildlife Reserve in Norfolk (England) take inspiration from American prairie landscapes. Their swaths and drifts avoid formal geometries, and, although carefully contrived, have a spontaneous air. They also favour local ecosystems. .

RIGHT At the Sedelle Arboretum, in the Limousin (France), over a hundred maple taxons settle happily into a wild valley which mixes marshland, meadow and wooded slopes. Everything evolves beautifully in the hands of Philippe and Nell Wanty, Franco-New Zealander plant lovers.

What landscape model inspires or informs this garden? Natural gardens of all persuasions aim to 'intensify a natural ambience and to condense and underline a theme derived from nature herself'.[67] Gardeners inspired by idealized countryside or abandoned farmland make wildflower meadows. Forests are distilled into 'woodland' gardens; the American Midwest features prairie gardens; German designers imitate the steppe; Mediterraneans make *garigue* gardens. Where the model is local, critics complain that such a garden is indistinguishable from the surrounding landscape, at best an improved concentration.[68] Where the gardener works mainly to support existing ecosytems, or where the illusion is perfectly contrived, newcomers may feel some confusion. At Lunuganga in Sri Lanka, a visitor to Geoffrey Bawa's magnificent site, beautifully arranged to appear spontaneous, exclaimed: 'This would be a lovely place to have a garden!'[69]

The Home Farm project in the centre of England was crucial to the designer Dan Pearson's earliest explorations of naturalistic, sustainable plantings. Pearson blurs boundaries with the surrounding landscape (furrowed fields and woodland), bringing countryside into the garden.

OPPOSITE At the Bloedel Reserve and
Wildlife Sanctuary in Washington State
(USA), the distinguished landscape architect
Richard Haag used minimal but powerful
intervention to celebrate natural landscapes,
including this rainforest moss garden,
under a canopy of *Aralia spinosa*.

BELOW At the Jardins Clos de la Forge in
the Limousin (France), Christian Allaert
and Jacques Sautot have developed
several small wild spaces, each with its own
character but all 'in movement', like the
Valley of ecologist Gilles Clément, nearby
[p. 130]. Such gardens not only blend with,
they are ever-changing enrichments of
local landscapes.

How are transitions managed towards the world outside? Are
the borders hidden, as in the garden of Heidi Gildemeister in
Mallorca [p. 162], where spontaneous growth, arranged and
enriched, merges first into a sheep park, then into a magnificent
mountain setting? Her invisible fencing, necessary to keep
livestock at bay, functions like the 'ha-ha' (invisible ditch) of
18th-century landscape parks.[70] In urban centres or industrial
zones, however, where the 'natural' garden contrasts strongly
with its environment, boundaries are clearly defined. One
ecological garden network in Holland is called 'Oase' (oases).[71]
In Germany, some bombed city centres have become 'naturalistic'
parks. In other examples, islands of industrial wasteland have
been reclaimed for nature (by Richard Haag in the US, Latz and
Partners in Germany). How have the history and former usage
of this site contributed to determining its boundaries?

From what distance, what points of view, do you experience this garden? Natural gardens can be unsettling. They often challenge conventional ways of imposing limits, defining perspectives and points of view, framing scenes or establishing a comfortable sense of scale. In today's ecologically inspired versions, you become immersed in the living substance, getting down on hands and knees to examine a spider web. Nor is sight the only sense engaged: you sniff, touch and listen as you observe ecosystems evolving. Mind and eye discover constantly; you look down, up, at close detailing or a vast horizon. Your active participation is usually required, and a sense of wonder replaces aesthetic admiration from a safe distance. Gilles Clément writes, 'My gardens are meant to be brushed against' [pp. 99, 130, 131].[72]

Are there obvious shapes, lines and forms – geometric patterning, straight lines or symmetry, curves and biomorphic forms? Straight lines, for 'Capability' Brown as for Jean-Jacques Rousseau, were 'the enemy of nature and diversity'. Right angles are traditionally imposed on human living spaces by buildings and walks, artificial constructs necessary for human use. Natural garden makers who wish to minimize human presence use only paths which are curved, sunken, raised, multiple or scarcely there at all. Dwellings are buried, smothered in vegetation, turned into tree houses, or put somewhere else. Those who accept that *Homo sapiens* also belongs to the biosphere admit human habitat and trails as much as those of other fauna. The Norwegian-American modernist Garrett Eckbo already queried: 'Why must we be naturalistic or formal? What about the gradations in between? The fallacious nature vs. man concept . . . isn't it time to put man and nature back together again?'[73]

Visionary projects at Westpark in Munich (Germany) allowed designers to experiment with steppe-inspired, drought-tolerant plantings on poor, stony soil. Such schemes by Rosemarie Weisse, determined by rigorous ecological observation, have proved a powerful model internationally.

Are the plants found in this garden those which grow wild locally, or do they come from far away? 'Native' versus 'exotic' plants – the quarrel rages. The English horticulturalist William Robinson, in his influential book *The Wild Garden* (1870), welcomed exotics as well as British flora. Today in the US, South Africa, Australia and New Zealand, many gardeners feel that only native plants are truly trouble-free. But native to where? This beach, this town, this region? And native since when? Before the last Ice Age in Europe? Before European colonization elsewhere? If imported plants need so much nurturing, why are they rejected as potentially invasive? American experts debating at the Brooklyn Botanic Garden decided to judge plants on their behaviour, not their origins.[74] Diversity remains the first priority. Non-specialist garden visitors will have trouble telling natives from imports and be happy as long as the general impression is harmonious. 'The main objective', writes Clément, 'is to encourage biological diversity, a source of wonder and our guarantee for the future.'[75]

At his estate near Rio de Janeiro in Brazil, Sitio Santo Antonio da Bica in Campo Grande, Roberto Burle Marx (1909–94) beautifully combined on 198 acres (80 hectares) more than 3,500 species, many from nearby virgin rainforests. As a student, he had observed that Brazilian gardeners then prized only European plants, while European botanists treasured Brazilian natives.

How are plants grouped together in this garden? British, Dutch and German 'naturalistic' designers recommend techniques like 'matrix' plantings to concentrate the 'visual impact' of wild landscapes in smaller gardens.[76] Grasses and bulbs intermingle with perennials and annuals (discrete colours, single blossoms, graphic seed heads). Larger shrubs and trees are pruned only to maintain the desired balance of sun and shade. Such methods, though sometimes labour-intensive, create beautiful effects. Ecologists proposing minimal intervention accept 'messier' results. The Dutch garden-maker Henk Gerritsen [*pp. 64–65*] observes: 'Wild plants in nature don't grow in a disorderly mish-mash, but are grouped three-dimensionally in recognizable plant communities and in harmony with the scenery.'[77] Gilles Clément concurs: 'Biological order implies a precise behavioural sequence as species evolve through time. It is rigorous according to its own terms, but in formal terms it looks like disorder.'[78] Empathetic visitors learn to look with different eyes.

What cultural methods are used in this garden? 'Natural' gardening implies a concern for energy in all its forms. Ecologically guided management aims to maintain and improve the biological potential of soil, water and air while limiting the use of machinery. Local materials needing minimum transportation are recommended. Water is used in the most sparing way. All natural gardeners concur in rejecting lawns as greedy in resources and a threat to biodiversity. Ecology and economy are always closely linked: recycling is the essence of natural gardening, beginning with composting and home-made plant concoctions like nettle broth to feed and protect plants. Organic food production may also contribute to this frugal way of life. Is this garden – and perhaps its owner – tired-looking, or bursting with vitality? Does this depend on the day, the season? Do moral and practical criteria count more here than good looks?

The owners of Brenthurst Gardens in Johannesburg (South Africa) boast of its being a forest with garden clearings. Begun in 1906, the estate gardens have evolved more and more towards 'natural' style and management, particularly as regards water.

OPPOSITE Lady Farm in Somerset (England) is a blend of cottage and steppe or prairie gardening, begun in 1992 by Judy and Malcolm Pearce. A dry, south-facing slope with sparse soil has become the garden's best-known feature. In Britain, purely native planting is not viable, and South African *Kniphofia* are welcomed here.

What role does the gardener play here? Natural management implies a gardener with an intimate knowledge of local ecosystems, for whom intervention is part of ongoing process. Such gardeners welcome, indeed depend upon, other species. Are there bird houses here, special passages for amphibians as in many Dutch gardens, plantings for insects and butterflies? Visitors see only a moment in the natural garden's ongoing evolution. Is the intended direction evident? How can you know that a particular stand of 'weeds' is there to provide food for a particular species of butterfly? In some public parks today, it is not the designer but the gardeners themselves who 'steer the natural process of succession', a practice begun in Holland decades ago. In the 'moving' (i.e. evolving) garden at the Parc Citroën in Paris, paths are remade yearly, simply by mowing around self-sown wildflowers. It is the park's gardeners who observe and decide on the layout from season to season. Natural gardening often suggests spontaneity rather than a pre-established concept or plan.

The French gardener Gilles Clément, ecologist, philosopher and designer of numerous parks worldwide, built his house himself at the Valley in the Creuse (France) on abandoned farmland where he once observed wildlife as a child. His 'moving' approach has developed into a working model for sustainable, planet-friendly gardening.

Is the garden you are visiting connected to some larger network – through neighbouring properties, associations, shared philosophical vision? For many 19th-century Romantics, nature offered solitary refuge from corrupt society. Today, natural gardening often brings people together. Individual properties may link up directly with the neighbours. In some American suburbs where lawns used to flow continuously from yard to yard, whole communities have switched to wildlife gardening, a change much appreciated by fauna needing trails throughout a territory. Many gardeners belong to associations promoting conservation, organic agriculture, heirloom seed saving, etc. The smallest garden is felt to engage the future of the planet. As the British designer Noel Kingsbury puts it: 'As the garden, so the earth.'[79]

Gardens in homage to the 18th-century ecologist Jean-Baptiste Lamarck at Valloires Abbey in Picardy (France) begin with a spiral featuring prehistoric vegetation and show plant evolution up the hill, towards modern times. They were designed by Gilles Clément and Miguel Georgieff.

TWO VIEWS

I began to roam ecstatically through this orchard thus metamorphosed, and although I did not find exotic plants and products of the Indies, I found the local ones arranged and combined in a manner that yielded a cheerier and pleasanter effect. The verdant grass, lush, but short and thick, was mingled with wild thyme, balsam, garden thyme, marjoram and other aromatic herbs. A thousand wild flowers shone there, among which the eye was surprised to detect a few garden varieties, which seemed to grow naturally with the others ... Nowhere do I see the slightest trace of cultivation. Everything is verdant, fresh, vigorous, and the gardener's hand is not to be seen. Nothing belies the idea of a desert island which came to my mind as I entered, and I see no human footprints. Ah, said Monsieur de Wolmar, that is because we have taken great pains to erase them. I have sometimes been witness and sometimes accomplice to the trickery ...

Jean-Jacques Rousseau, *Julie, or The New Héloïse*, 1761[80]

Wild gardening for Robinson was a way of leavening garden starchiness with the treasures and intrinsic spontaneity of a still comparatively unplundered nature. It wouldn't have occurred to him that gardens might one day be last-ditch refuges for the endangered qualities of 'wildness' ... two of his best-loved flowers, golden rod and Michaelmas daisy, thrown out of gardens precisely because their powers of naturalization are a sight too wild for most gardeners, have taken up residence on mainline railway embankments, and are now spreading in spectacular, mottled, billowing sheets – exactly how their champion felt they should be.

Richard Mabey, introduction to William Robinson's *The Wild Garden*[81]

For Wigandia, his highly original garden in Victoria (Australia), William Martin chose only plants adapted to extreme growing conditions on the side of an extinct volcano, and which blend in with the unusual surroundings. Dramatic foliage and form count here more than flower.

Ten Questions for Personal and Home Gardens

And then, what is a 'personal' garden? It is a garden at the home of the owner, designer and principal maintainer and shows unmistakable signs of private passion. It is often delightfully idiosyncratic.

Anne Wareham, of Veddw House Garden in Wales[82]

Let no one imagine that real gardening is some sort of bucolic or contemplative activity. It is an unquenchable passion, like anything else that concerns serious people.

Karel Capek, *The Gardener's Year*, 1929

Who made this garden, who works in it, whose personality has stamped it? Do its owners make most or all decisions about design and maintenance? How much time do they spend in their garden? Who actually does the hands-in-dirt work? If a professional has played a part here, were you told this? Gardens with character can result from fruitful dialogue between owners and designer, but not if the designer has merely been hired to imprint the garden with a fashionably flaunted 'signature'. Gertrude Jekyll defined the personal garden a hundred years ago: 'The size of a garden has very little to do with its merit. It is merely an accident relating to the circumstances of the owner. It is the size of his heart and brain and goodwill that will make his garden either delightful or dull, as the case may be, and either leave it at the monotonous, dead level, or raise it, in whatever degree he may, towards that of a work of fine art.'[83]

The American architect Jim Thompson began creating his house and garden in Bangkok (Thailand) in 1959, combining traditional Thai architecture and lush tropical vegetation. He often entertained in the garden, now part of a trust and museum.

<small>PREVIOUS PAGES</small>

<small>LEFT</small> Great Dixter in Sussex (England) was the family home of Christopher Lloyd (1921–2007), whose strong personality, expressed both in the garden and in his many books, made it perhaps the best-known and most influential garden in Britain of the late 20th century.

<small>RIGHT</small> Nicole de Vésian made her garden in Provence (France) in barely ten years, but its use of clipped evergreen foliage to define small spaces [*see also p. 154*] has since been imitated all over the world. Christopher Lloyd wrote of her: 'Such an individualist! That is rare and a treat when met.'

Did discernible influences or models inspire this garden? Can you easily detect the style of a certain television programme or magazine? or perhaps a foreign model – English gardens in Australia, or Italian parterres in California? New gardeners are often unsure of themselves. The American designer Bunny Williams advises clients to travel, consult books and magazines, even to look at the clothes in their closet to get a sense of their own personal style.[84] The goal is assimilation, not exact imitation of a model or a ragbag of styles – unless pastiche is the point of the garden! Personal gardens are not necessarily private. Very original gardens have been made to please the visiting public. Nonetheless, the Australian writer Michael McCoy experienced an identity crisis after designing a garden entirely in terms of visitor expectations: 'the needs of the garden visitor started slowly and insidiously to dominate my own', he noted, and he ended up wondering: 'Can I now claim this garden back as my own?'[85]

Great Dixter's head gardener, Fergus Garrett, another strong personality, is also chief executive of the Great Dixter Charitable Trust, which aims to keep Christopher Lloyd's work alive. Visitors often used to meet the writer himself gardening in the borders.

Sensitive designers like Julie Toll (based in England) help owners work out what they really want and avoid pitfalls, as architects do in building. Designers may be artists whose works are gardens. Many of the world's most beautiful gardens are the result of creative efforts thus combined – owner's and designer's.

How old is this garden, and how is it evolving and changing? Does it include historic vestiges? Bits left over from previous owners? Was it assembled very quickly, or is its present state the result of long ripening, incorporating many changes, perhaps even catastrophes? Heidi Gildemeister writes: 'I like gardens where I feel the presence of the "creator" and preferably visit it together with him/her; where plans for the future are interesting; where the owners are happy with what has been achieved – without discussing at length their failures, often imaginary ones; where the owner is in harmony with the garden.' The American writer Henry Mitchell, thinking of the accidents which affect all gardens, goes so far as to claim: 'If I see a garden that is very beautiful, I know it is a new garden!' But he adds: 'It is not important for a garden to be beautiful. It is extremely important for the gardener to think it a fair substitute for Eden.'[86] Personal gardens may require tolerance from visitors about jobs not yet tended to, or plans only half realized.

Helen Dillon's highly personal garden in Dublin, in the Republic of Ireland, is an icon today, familiar to a wide public through her lectures and books. She combines colourful plant collections with strong design centred on a series of pools, canals and cascades.

What are the growing conditions in this garden? What are its climate zone, prevailing winds, the composition of its soil, annual rainfall, topography, drainage . . . ? If this information is not obvious, usually the owner will happily provide it. Does the garden adapt to these conditions or fight them, and if the latter, how is battle waged and who is winning? Is upkeep relaxed, episodic, compulsive? The Canadian writer Jennifer Bennett tells us: 'I am impressed by gardeners who don't panic about weeds, although it seems that weeds do not take over their gardens. I am impressed by gardens that allow visitors to linger, with maybe a bench or chairs. These gardens may be spectacular in spots and at certain times of year, or they may not. What they offer is adventure and a sense of calm and welcome.'[87]

How is space divided in this garden, and does it tell a story? First of all, what area does it cover? Is it walled in, or partly or entirely open to the surrounding landscape? Is the garden mainly an extension of the house, the famous 'outdoor room'? Is it divided internally by paths, walls, objects, hedging? Are its parts well proportioned, clearly defined, visible from each other, half smothered, completely separate, or overlapping? Have the owners used professional tricks to make a small garden look bigger (diminishing intervals between plants in a row, for example, or through colour choices)? Have they deliberately distorted scale? Some professionals, like Michel Semini in Provence [*pp. 151, 161*], feel that crowding a small space makes it seem bigger, while others prefer immediate readability. What is the balance here between coherence and mystery? Sometimes the garden is clearly autobiographical, its parts corresponding to chapters in a life. This usually involves big properties which tell their story through a sequence of different 'rooms'.

The Laskett, in Herefordshire (England), was begun over thirty years ago by Sir Roy Strong and Dr Julia Trevelyan Oman. Much of the garden is biographical, referring to happenings and characters in their eventful lives given over largely to art and theatre.

OPPOSITE La Mortella at Ischia (Italy) bears the mark, first of all, of the international designer Russell Page, then of its owner, Lady Walton, an adventurous plantswoman who today arranges concerts of her composer husband's music in these gardens. Ferny pools and grottoes offer more intimate spaces.

OPPOSITE The designer Raymond Jungles, based in Florida (USA), loves to use dramatic tropical foliage plants and water features in his designs. His own garden is inspired by South American rainforests and the work of the Brazilian artist Roberto Burle Marx [pp. 126–27, 186].

RIGHT The personal garden of Hugues Peuvergne, a young French designer with many original ideas, who first became a gardener so he could live and work outdoors. He likes to experiment with unusual dwellings made with bales of straw or leafy boughs, and peoples them with exotic presences.

Where do the plants come from and how were they chosen?

Are the owners the kind who cannot resist new plants even when there is no more room? Perfectionists who arrange carefully balanced pictures with colours and shapes, foliage and flower? Do they produce plants themselves from seed or cuttings? Use gifts from friends and neighbours? check out garden centre specials? bring home souvenirs from trips? Are the plants rare or commonplace? Do they make the owners happy? Virgil wrote already in the 3rd century BC: 'I saw an old man of Corcyus, who owned some few acres of waste land, a field neither rich for grazing nor favourable to the flock nor apt for the vineyard; yet he, setting thinly sown garden-stuff among the brushwood, with borders of white lilies and vervain and the seeded poppy, equalled in his content the wealth of kings.'[88]

How are the plants assembled, according to what criteria? The designer Russell Page suggested that garden makers and visitors consider questions about colour contrasts, the size of planting blocks, the use of 'clear shapes' or 'broken wavering masses'. Numerous books help gardeners calculate plants per area with graded heights. In this garden, is success totally equated with plantsmanship? A famous and very personal perennial garden was created by Sandra and Nori Pope at Hadspen in England. When they retired as tenants, the owner of the space, Niall Hobhouse, razed it and commissioned Foreign Office Architects to develop a 'design concept' – a layout. An international competition then solicited innovative 'design', by which was meant mainly planting schemes. Many proposals were in fact conceptualist, using features like sunken walls, contrasting angles of vision, lines and patterns of trees, 'a rhythm of pathways', 'sequential drifts' and 'user-created content'.[89] These contestants refused to separate structure and horticulture expertise.

In Berkeley, California (USA), the artists Martha Donahue and Mark Bulwinkle live surrounded by the 'Our Own Stuff' Gallery Garden where they present their 'yard art'. Objects and plants blend into a nearly impenetrable tapestry, full of delights and surprises. Long perspectives are few, but striking when they occur.

The writer Anne Wareham and the photographer Charles Hawes, although expert with plants, like a more adventuresome approach in their garden at Veddw House in Wales. They use the term 'modern romantic', while others deem this one of Britain's most original creations.

What buildings, constructions, and objects play a role in this garden?
Often objects come from junk shops or are home-made with recycled materials. Are they useful? funny? historic? symbolic like Ian Hamilton Finlay's famous submarine conning tower at Little Sparta in Scotland? Are objects and constructions here intrusive or discrete? A shout or a whisper?[90] How are they placed? Are they there mainly for the owners' pleasure, to enhance visitor enjoyment or impress? Do visitors appreciate them or find them an embarrassment? Anne Wareham complains: 'Our objects have the curious habit of becoming invisible when people visit. Visitors will walk right past an inscribed headstone, or a profile of a buzzard, and they clearly cannot see them. It is possible that it is because the headstones and buzzards are so embarrassingly awful, but we get quite a lot of visitors and you might think that there might be some with the same gruesome bad taste as ourselves. But it may just be that that they only see the plants.'[91]

Do you feel that this garden is a place of growth and life? Winston
Churchill is quoted as saying that war is man's natural element.
And then adding: 'War and gardening.' Gardens are by definition
life-giving, but most chemicals sold to home gardeners were
first invented for warfare and are intended to kill, proving lethal
sometimes both to gardeners and to their environment. Today
'biodiversity' is the catchword, an affirmation of life in all forms,
including the gardener's. The French philosopher-gardener
Anne Cauquelin sums up thus: 'Gardens offer day-to-day magic:
wonderment survives routine wear-and-tear, enjoyment emerges
from hard work and impulsive pleasure from the hoeing of a long,
hard row.'[92] Good taste counts less than vitality. The American
writer Henry Mitchell recounts that people are always asking him
if they may plant a magenta azalea. He encourages them to add
red tulips as well, concluding: 'A garden is more than a matter of
the right fish fork, as it were.'[93]

Would you say this is an eccentric's creation, or an artist's garden?
Expressive personality has long been associated with both
eccentricity and art – at Las Pozas in Mexico, for example, or the
'castle' of the Facteur Cheval in France. Perhaps the garden is
already recognized as the work of a famous artist, like Monet's
Giverny [*opposite*], Derek Jarman's beach garden at Dungeness in
England, or Finlay's Little Sparta [*p. 105*]. It might be said that all
personal gardeners are artists. Thierry and Monique Dronet,
makers of Berchigranges in Lorraine [*p. 148*], admire 'living gardens
where the creators live deeply, always evolving . . . Gardens which
explore new ways, take risks, but remain in harmony with nature.
Gardens which let visitors make contact with nature. Gardens
which are created with feeling and communicate this. Usually
gardens created with few means because this promotes creativity!
Whatever the style, a garden made with love.'

Strong personality combined with
creative vision make gardeners into artists
and sometimes artists into gardeners.
Few scenes have so marked contemporary
taste as the 19th-century wisteria bridge
of the painter Claude Monet in his garden
at Giverny in Normandy (France).

TWO VIEWS

A garden like a life is composed of moments ... At the beginning when my garden was new and thoughts of it agitated my days and dreams, I kept inviting friends to come and see my back yard paradise. They'd stroll the gravel paths, duly appreciative of the flowers and vegetables but never, it seemed to me, enthusiastic enough. Was this because my garden was actually rather dull? Or were they blind to its true beauty and real fascination? Finally, I realized that what makes my garden exciting is ME. Living in it every day, participating minutely in each small event, I see with doubled and redoubled vision. Where friends notice a solitary hummingbird pricking the salvia flowers, I'll recall a season's worth of hummingbird battles. Where they see an ordinary mocking bird, I know a distinct individual whom I've studied as a forager, fighter, performer. My friends, present in the garden only transiently, notice the surface prettiness, admire, and pass on to matters of more substance. While I see not merely the garden at this particular moment, but the garden as it has been at all other moments, and as it will be in moments yet to come.

Janet Emily Bowers, contemporary American author[94]

I have no special admiration for the gardens of the aristocracy, some of which are beautiful, others not. Still less do I value money-power in any department of life, and the gardens of the very rich are often the worst. But I am snobbish about the banal, and when I see a planting which is so frequently used as to be utterly boring, I want to avoid it. The common dismissive word for such planting is 'suburban', but this is unfair to the suburbs, which are inhabited by some of the best gardeners in Britain. The word has taken off because sometimes all the gardeners in a street or district tend to copy one another, and you see the same Kanzan cherry trees, the same camellias, the same hybrid tea roses repeated until they become a cliché. I think that my objection to my pink prunus with daffodils is of snobbish rather than aesthetic origin. They might look well together if one saw this combination of pastels for the first time ... I defend garden snobbery if it makes you use your own eyes instead of copying fashionable ideas.

Anne Scott-James, *Gardening Letters to my Daughter*, 1991[95]

To create the gardens at Berchigranges, in Lorraine (France), Thierry and Monique Dronet cleared an abandoned mountain quarry, cutting down three thousand fir trees. Today, many different ambiences and four thousand plant varieties provide visitors with much delight from season to season.

Ten Questions for Gardens of Mediterranean Inspiration

… the familiar prospects of vines, olives, cypresses; one comes to believe that they are Platonic abstractions rooted in the imagination of man. Symbols of the Mediterranean, they are always here to welcome one … the enchanted landscapes of the European heart.

Lawrence Durrell, 'Across Secret Provence', 1969[96]

… structures, made of local materials, economically apt, fit in well with local climate, flora, fauna, ways of life … Human in scale, they have a sensual frugality that results in true elegance.

Victor Papanek, *The Green Imperative*, 1995[97]

In what sense is this garden 'Mediterranean'? Does it grow near Mediterranean shores or in a comparable climate zone, between temperate and subtropical, with long, hot, dry summers and heavy rainfall in autumn and winter (in south-west Australia, Chile, South Africa, California perhaps)? Do olive trees thrive here year round? Do citrus? Does intense, dry, summer sunshine give rich flavour to fruit, vegetables, oils and wine? Or is it a temperate zone garden where special microclimates (city courtyards for example) allow the growing of semi-hardy 'Mediterranean' plants? Perhaps it simply has a 'Mediterranean' décor – lavenders, terracotta pots – expressing holiday nostalgia? Mediterranean gardens are by definition multicultural and global, so much so that some reject the very term as too specifically European. Whatever it is called, the style combines global distribution with infinite local variations. But, like Mediterranean cuisine with which it is closely linked, the Mediterranean garden has a logic of its own.

Has this land been used for farming, and is it still productive in any way? Many homes in Mediterranean climates were originally farms. Their use today by city people is not new: Pliny the Younger, in the late 1st century AD, made his famous country gardens for escape from duties in Rome.[98] More recent landed gentry kept townhouses while living off their farming estates. Mediterranean tradition never separated elegance from abundance, beauty and productivity. A suitor in Boccaccio's *Decameron* (1342) sends his lady a 'few cloves of fresh garlic of which he grew the finest specimens thereabouts in his own garden'![99] 'Splendid' Florentine villas, wrote Edith Wharton in the early 20th century, 'stood close-set among their olive-orchards and vineyards.'[100] Today wine properties from California to Australia, South Africa or Provence renew this heritage. Even the smallest Mediterranean garden has a fruit tree or vine. These pleasure places for family and friends adapt well to today's ideals of sustainability and use of local resources. The symbol of this ideal blending of use and beauty, worshipped at times to the point of fetish, is the olive tree.

PREVIOUS PAGES

LEFT The tiny seaside garden of Mireille Ferrari in the Var, on the French Riviera, combines common wildflowers with horticultural treasures, driftwood, and playful pruning. Most everything built uses recycled materials. This garden is also a refuge for local wildlife.

RIGHT The designer Michel Semini, working in Provence (France), tries to convince his Parisian film and fashion clients to plant olive trees with santolina circles rather than lush lawn. For Mediterraneans, the olive tree is a symbol: beautiful and fruitful living sculpture admirably suited to local landscapes and climate.

Mediterranean gardens were once dismissed as too productive to be ornamental. Today – as in ancient times – farm and wine properties often have admirable gardens. The Rustenberg Estate in South Africa produces Stellenbosch wines and has been receiving visitors since 1682.

How are house and garden related by the logic of place? 'The garden was bounded on one side by the house, from which it flowed and into which it ran', wrote the American novelist F. Scott Fitzgerald at Cap d'Antibes around 1930.[101] The 'outdoor room' has ancient Mediterranean variants: courtyards, enclosed or half open; arbours and trellises extending the building. Different exposures invite outdoor eating throughout the day and the year. Vernacular architecture and plantings have always collaborated in climate management: a house sits under the crest and not right on top of the hill, turning its back to prevailing winds, facing the sun. Its hedges and copses serve as windbreaks. Big deciduous trees shade it in summer but let in winter sun. Climbers and vines insulate the walls, often very thick with small openings. They must not interfere with shutters which, carefully regulated, keep indoor temperatures even in all seasons. This logic of place depends on the thrifty management of natural energies – wind, sun and water – for maximum profit and pleasure.

How does this garden relate to the landscape beyond? Is its site flat or steep, open or enclosed? Irregular topography lets most Mediterranean-style gardens look beyond walls, at least from a roof or upper storey, though city courtyards and Islamic gardens may open only to the sky. Hillside terracing lets a garden be both sheltered and open. Old farming estates sit among their valley lands like the yolk of an egg, their parterres echoing surrounding field patterns. Their vistas are not 'borrowed'; rather countryside naturally extends the garden in a series of planes from near to far, a feature already appreciated by Pliny. In parts of Spain and North Africa, the view may be from a roof terrace. In built-up areas like the Riviera and parts of California, gardens become secret oases; remaining views are framed like a flat and distant cinema screen, the middle ground carefully blocked out.

The fashion designer Nicole de Vésian restored her house in Provence (France) to frame the garden and planned the garden with graded views towards the landscapes beyond [see also p. 135]. Everything is both intimate and open, spontaneous and controlled but never regimented.

On a much vaster scale, the English designer Tim Rees also created graded views starting from a house terrace (shaded by 17th-century plane trees) passing over lavender fields and manmade wildflower meadows to the wooded skyline of the Alpilles hills in Provence (France).

How is space organized here, and on what scale? Views composed
of a series of planes from house to horizon have their vertical
counterpart: plantings are layered from low evergreen shrubberies
to canopies of deciduous trees, orchestrating year-round climate
control. Open areas are usually paved or gravel-covered house
terraces or courtyards (English-style lawn is an import, though
a relatively old one). Sitting and walking areas remain intimate;
around them, grey or green shrubs are mounded and grouped
from low to higher, with candle cypress or other fastigiates,
sculpture or pots as accents. Arbours and smaller trees extend
overhead, shading walks and sometimes even parterres in
summer. This sense of enclosure differs from broad English
lawns, or Japanese miniaturization, or the vast wild spaces of
the Americas and Australia. Mediterranean cultural traditions
are sometimes called 'humanist' in part because of this human
scale used in spatial organization.

The Provençal artist Dominique Lafourcade,
faced with flat land, created green, three-
dimensional patterns around a rill. In her
region, *Viburnum laurustinus* is the preferred
plant for clipping. In northern Spain
Fernando Caruncho likes escallonia, while
Heidi Gildemeister in Mallorca uses wild
Pistachia lentiscus.

The Provençal plant sculptor Marc Nucera invented 'Walkers' from upturned oak trunks placed in semi-wild meadowland at the Mas Benoît. His art always involves the past history and present character of related landscape.

What plants are used here, how, and why? Are the plants here lush or the kind that thrive emerging from cracks between rocks? Mediterranean 'natives' adapt to dry climates and sparse, poor soil as bulbs, annuals, woody subshrubs with leathery, spiky or thorny foliage rich with aromatic oils. But perhaps acclimatizing rare exotics is the whole point of the garden? Or perhaps the broad-leafed evergreens which thrive here have been clipped to define space and catch the brilliant light? Each region seems to have a favourite, basic building plant – box, pistachia, laurustinus, rosemary, escallonia, or laurel, for example. But whether planty, architectural, sculptural, or all three at once, a Mediterranean garden will have year-round interest because fruit and foliage (green, grey or mixed) count as much as floral display. Flowers mainly provide accents, in all seasons. Visual appeal may count most, but not exclusively. Fragrance is usually intense, with tactile appeal as well. Such pleasure gardens do not keep you at a distance and may even overpower.

An influential pioneer in waterwise techniques was Beth Chatto, whose Gravel Garden in Essex, begun in the 1970s (OPPOSITE), was inspired by a New Zealand landscape. But already in the 1950s, Californian Ruth Bancroft was experimenting at Walnut Creek with cactus, aloes, agaves, bromeliaceae and many other xerophytes (ABOVE). Today's champions, who stress the delights rather than the constraints of dry gardening, are Heidi Gildemeister of Mallorca, in Spain [p. 162], and Olivier Filippi, in the Languedoc in France [p. 164].

What kind of light does this garden enjoy at different times of day and year? How does it affect colours, shapes and textures? 'Mediterranean' for most people evokes sunshine, hot and intense, and vast blue skies. Broadleaf evergreen foliage lends itself to sculpting light, theatrical contrasts. Weathered stone, terracotta, furry grey foliage absorb light, while leathery leaf surfaces, glazed tiles and water reflect it. Good garden design orchestrates texture as well as colour. Some gardeners like bright, festive, holiday colours in hot climates, but others prefer greys and pastels, taking olive foliage and silver limestone as the keynote. Ochre and terracotta tones in pots, paving or whole buildings may add warm accents to 'green' or 'grey' gardens. Light sculpting form also links up to an ancient metaphysical heritage influencing contemporary designers like the Spaniard Fernando Caruncho [p. 161], who explains: 'I strive to arrange a space that invites reflection and inquiry by allowing the light to delineate geometries, and this way discover the dynamic symmetries of nature.'[102]

Classic and neoclassic Mediterranean gardens often make a showcase of water. In Spain, Fernando Caruncho, inspired perhaps by farm reservoirs and the Mexican architect Luis Barragán, designs beautifully minimalist reflecting pools (OPPOSITE). Michel Semini creates intimate swimming pools that look like elegant garden features – here for Pierre Bergé, in Provence, France (BELOW).

Where does the water come from, how is it managed and used?

Water, the subject of disputes for centuries, illustrates better than anything else the Mediterranean blending of frugal necessity and pleasure. Stone – heavy, immobile, weathered – often serves as a foil for water's quick, light-catching movement, from mountain cascades and ancient irrigation canals to elaborate fountains. Is water in this garden a baroque, extravagant show, a minimalist reflective surface, a wildlife pond? Or is this garden an example of today's 'waterless' approach, inspired by the successful ecosystems of dry scrubland, maquis or garigue? The current mix of economy, elegance, enjoyment and ecological awareness offers a new development on old Mediterranean themes.[103]

What is old here, and what is new; and how old, how new?

'Mediterranean' for many implies 'ancient': Lawrence Durrell in Corfu praised the 'pungent smell' of black olives as 'a taste older than meat, older than wine. A taste as old as cold water.'[104] Does this garden deliberately evoke such images? Californians look to Spanish colonial, Provençal owners display genuine Roman ruins – which Greeks find 'new'! Mediterranean minimalists hark back to Platonic ideas in their exploration of natural form. More prosaically, jetset owners wanting instant gardens pay fortunes to transplant five-hundred-year-old olive trees. Decorators carefully distress wood and stone, rub paint off new shutters, and hide modern technology. Peasant logic applied to home gardening suggests another approach: careful observation of what is already on site with a view to preserving and recycling. Even dead trees can become sculpture. Imagination replaces expense.

In her brilliant garden on a sheep farm in Mallorca (Spain), Heidi Gildemeister clips often to maintain graded perspectives. Rare imported plants thrive amidst spontaneous growth, hard to distinguish, just as built and natural formations are hard to tell apart. 'Wild' and 'shaped' are a continuum, not in opposition.

The sculptor Alain David Idoux created original landscape art set against dramatic crags at the Mas Benoît in Provence (France). His work renews those Mediterranean 'traditions of beauty, discipline, frugality and artistic patience' admired by the English writer Ford Madox Ford in 1935.

How wild, natural, or formal is this garden? Natural water, stone, and broadleaf evergreens, in human hands, become irrigation, sustaining walls, windbreak hedges. Pushed further, as fountains and pools, balustrades, sculpture, parterres and topiary, they may be works of art. Outside the garden, manmade constructions and eroded cliffs are hard to distinguish. Wind pressure produces globes and mounds plants naturally. Pruning, at its best, is both a farm technique and an art, producing shade, windbreaks, fruit, wine – and beauty. This ancient intimacy of the neat and the rude makes Mediterranean landscapes ideal sites for contemporary land art – as Finlay [*cf. p. 105*] and Goldsworthy [*p. 111*] both discovered in Provence. Dialogue, not domination, is the aim: a climate capable of destroying a vineyard in minutes can never be controlled. Medieval troubadours in Languedoc praised a courtly virtue they called 'mesura' – measure, or 'form'. It is perhaps in this sense that Mediterranean gardens are deeply 'formal', even the wildest among them, but also deeply natural, like courtly love.

TWO VIEWS

In the summer, the wheat is tall and golden and the great plots sway gently in the wind. There is fruit in the orchard. Autumn brings the grape harvest and the cutting of the wheat. In winter the earth is plowed and sown and marked by wonderful patterns. And in the spring, once again, all is a sea of green. What could be more ennobling than producing flour from the wheat, wine from the vines, oil from the olives, and fruit from the trees? In a sense this is the first garden with all the purity of a Platonic ideal.

Fernando Caruncho, *Mirrors of Paradise*, 2000[105]

This little garden is a charming place where use and beauty are inseparable ! A garden full of attractions, which offers joy, shelter, food and relief from anxiety. A reinvigorating garden which captivates the eye. The work it requires is paid back a hundredfold! The person who cultivates it knows a thousand kinds of happiness !

Virgil, 'The Little Garden', from the *Catalects*, 1st century BC[106]

The French plant hunter Olivier Filippi scouted the world, then tested his best finds at his nursery in the Languedoc (France) before writing his seminal *Dry Gardening Handbook*. He finds that Mediterranean plants need sharp drainage and often grow best in poor soil with little water and a gravel mulch.

Ten Questions for Gardens of Japanese Inspiration

*The purpose of Japanese garden art is to create an image of Infinite Presence which is Nature,
with apparently limited means.*

Tsuyoshi Tamura, Japanese writer, 1935[107]

*Zen Garden: no flower, no path: where is man? In the carrying of the rocks, the raking
of the sand, the act of writing . . .*

Roland Barthes, French philosopher, 1970[108]

OPPOSITE Shisendo in Japan, one of
Kyoto's lesser-known stars, arranges azalea
globes with pink flowers in spring around
a sinuous path which constantly conceals,
then unveils, new scenes, in a series of
pictures. These gardens are particularly
linked to poetry and painting.

ABOVE Innisfree in New York State (USA),
the private garden of Walter and Marion Beck
(created 1930–60), embraces, the Webbs
explain, 'the Eastern design concept of
asymmetric balance that combines rhythm,
pattern, space and form'. Its artfully

arranged sequence deliberately evokes
both Japanese and Chinese models.

What was the original purpose of this garden and how is it used now? However small, the Japanese garden meets a deep spiritual need: it maintains human harmony with cosmic forces. All of its details have a ritual use. The great traditional gardens, closely linked to calligraphy, painting and poetry, were made for emperors and aristocrats ('lake-and-island' pleasure gardens) or monks (meditation temple gardens, country retreats which after 1600 became ceremonial tea gardens). For centuries, refined 'gentlemen of leisure' designed garden art implemented and maintained by a caste of artisan-gardeners. Tsuyoshi Tamura, writing for the Garden Club of America in 1935,[109] complained that Western fashions were promoting gardens as 'a pleasant place for rambling and exercise' or, worse, an 'outdoor living-room for women and children'! The challenge today is to combine various contemporary needs – both public and private – with the ancient spiritual function.

Daigo-ji in Kyoto, first established in 874, consecrated as a temple in 907, illustrates the early 'lake-and-island' style. It was restored in the 16th century and its cherry blossoms have been celebrated since that time.

Kamigamo-jinja is the oldest Shinto shrine in Kyoto, surrounded by sacred landscapes welcoming nature spirits. A summer harvest festival has been held here since the 6th century. It is said in Japan that Shintoism teaches the beginnings of man, Confucianism the middle, and Buddhism the end.

How does the local climate affect light, shadow and colours? Japanese writers link Zen meditation to 'Nature's twilight profundity'. 'Gloomy', 'dusky', 'murky' – these are all terms of praise.[110] The filtered light and mists of such a 'rain-washed' country inspire poetry celebrating moonlight and the sound of rain on foliage. Kyoto monastery gardens were re-sanded by moonlight, torrents directed to catch the moon's reflection.[111] Western mythologies seek light, cast out dark; here they are 'yin' and 'yang', the ink and the white page, fullness and void, both essential. Colours, especially in the Zen and tea gardens, are muted, worn or 'tarnished', bearing witness to slow weathering, a 'harmony of dusky green and grey welling out of their ancientness'.[112] 'This dusk is worth all the ornaments in the world', writes the essayist Junichiro Tanizaki.[113] White in the Japanese garden is soft: the rice and pebbles of Shinto shrines, moonlight, cherry petals or raked sand.

How are differences of scale used in this garden, and what vantage point do you perceive them from? Traditional Japanese gardens were experienced as 'miniature worlds of beauty' reproducing 'a symbolic space co-extensive with all heaven and earth',[114] whether they had lakes large enough for boating or were concentrated in a bonsai on a tray. Zen gardens use metaphor to produce quintessence – a stone is a mountain, raked sand becomes the ocean.[115] Such a garden was a picture to be contemplated in its entirety from a single viewpoint on the same level. Many contemporary Japanese homes still observe this plan: the garden is quietly appreciated from the living room. 'Stroll' and tea gardens – not domestic but religious categories – invite visitors to move ritualistically through garden space. Often a veranda or covered walkway offers pre-arranged viewpoints which change as you progress. Instead of one picture, you have a series on an unfolding scroll.[116]

The 15th-century Sesshu-in temple gardens in Kyoto, first made by the artist Oda Toyo, were restored in 1939 by Shigemori Mirei. The picturesque 'moon gate' adapted from Chinese models links indoors and out, night and day.

How is the garden space related to adjacent buildings and the landscape beyond? Traditionally, buildings and garden interpenetrate. There are covered walkways and garden pavilions in the lake and island parks and ceremonial tea-houses in the stroll gardens, while the sliding partitions of private homes make the garden an 'outdoor room' adaptable to shifting seasons. The garden is as important as the house, and has its own integrity.[117] The straight lines and right angles of architecture provide a necessary frame and backdrop for miniature landscapes that use mainly curves. Beyond the long straight back wall, however, rises the *shakkei*, the famous 'borrowed landscape' of trees or a mountain peak visible afar. In stroll gardens, this will be carefully framed by branches or other landscape features to create links between the near and the far. Are there 'views' here, and if so, how are they brought into the overall experience?

Ryoan-ji temple in Kyoto is best known for its 15th-century Zen garden. But its monastery verandas also frame other fine views, directing admiring attention from a precise vantage point, here towards brilliant autumn colour.

What kinds of paths are open to you and where do they take you?
The garden gate hides what is beyond but invites you to discover it.[118] Your freedom is limited, however: 'The direction of the circuit around the lake is always one way, and the viewer is not supposed to wander away from the footpath or to take wilfully the inverse course, since the composition is set in perfect accord with the circuit.'[119] The visit is a ritual, orchestrated like a piece of music which you would never play backwards or submit to individual variation. Yet you help perform it by accepting, for example, irregular stepping stones and curving paths that literally make you watch your step: walking in a Japanese-inspired garden is always 'a series of tests and sensations', says the French garden writer Jean-Paul Pigeat, who adds, 'the changes of direction to unveil something new are one of the Japanese garden's most profound features'.[120] Broad or long perspectives are excluded: 'In the Japanese garden the vista must be closed, so as to suggest the depth of the earth and the invisible distance of heaven.'[121]

BELOW The Saiho-ji in Kyoto, known as the Moss Temple, was founded in the 8th century, and reconstructed in the 12th and 14th centuries. The moss carpets of this large woodland garden cannot be walked on. Visitors keep to paths, following an established itinerary.

OPPOSITE At the John P. Humes Japanese Stroll Garden at Mill Neck, New York (USA), the designer Douglas DeFaya faithfully reproduced the uneven paving, almost monochrome colours, moist and filtered light, stone furnishings, and harmony with nature of its Japanese model.

What role does rockwork play in this garden? It is rockwork that 'tells most clearly the soul of the garden artist'.[122] Horizontal, vertical and diagonal placement is a question of period, type of garden, and the complex symbolism of yin and yang. Mineral elements vary from raked sand, pebble cascades, the graphic paving of Zen walkways to dramatic miniature stone mountains. Ceremonial tea gardens use more 'natural' rockwork, carefully evoking random strewing. Rocks are often brought from afar but must be set as they were, half buried, in their place of origin. The famous 12th-century gardening manual still used today, the *Sakutei-ki*, recommends: 'Do not place stones too abruptly, or with too much sophistication, but let them be a little bit vague.' Westerners unfamiliar with the religious context appreciate them as sculpture. But each remains individual; Western designers like Dan Pearson, working in Japan, find that drystone walls are an alien concept.[123]

Are there plants in this garden and if so, how are they used?
The mostly mineral Zen garden style [*pp. 176, 228–29*] remains intemporal, with moss at best, whereas the landscape, stroll or tea gardens [*pp. 172, 177, and opposite*] enjoy the rich symbolism of seasonal change – the pine and bamboo together in winter, for example.[124] Flowers, much loved in the art of Ikebana, are present in gardens mainly as shrubs and trees – peonies, azaleas, flowering cherries in spring, foliage colour in autumn, against a constant green background. Dwarf bamboos, moss, ivy, pachysandra, ferns, zoysias, etc., cover a garden floor rarely walked on. Conifers and broadleaf evergreens may be highly pruned – the first according to natural growth habit into 'clouds', the latter into waves and rounded shapes. Clipped greenery here catches raindrops, frost, and occasional snow. It helps define space, along with graphic plants such as bamboos, cycas, fatsias; but plant groupings also mark ritual passage of time. Each season has its complex symbols, again perceived by Westerners in purely aesthetic terms.

The landscape sculptor Erik Borja practices 'cloud' pruning in his Japanese–Mediterranean stroll garden in the Rhône valley (France). Western topiary, he feels, imposes shapes, whereas Japanese pruning opens up natural forms.

The Heian Jingu shrine in Kyoto was designed in the late 19th century by Ogawa Jihei in homage to traditional garden concepts. Stepping stones crossing the large pond require close attention to what is underfoot – a form of visitor participation.

How is water present, directed, enjoyed, symbolized? Waterscapes – calm or cascading – lend themselves to miniaturization, whether they suggest 'ocean, lake, pond, marsh or mere stream'. Points of origin and run-off are often included in the picture. Stones were traditionally selected for their capacity to evoke an ocean, river, mountain stream or marshland. The famous Zen dry gardens, the *kare-san-sui*, represent water with pebbles or sand, not from economy or conservation but as a higher degree of abstraction from the model, an evocation of life immobilized, eternalized. The inimitable Ryoan-ji in Kyoto, says the historian Michel Baridon, 'carries the spirit towards meditation as the Buddhists intended it, by raising the mind beyond the confusion of mere appearances'.[125]

BELOW The symbolic dry Zen gardens – here Taizo-in, Kyoto – reduce and abstract whole landscapes. Water is here represented by raked sand. Seasonal variation is excluded. But such miniaturization can in turn make space seem boundless, inviting meditation on the infinite.

OPPOSITE Stroll gardens and tea gardens welcome 'plants so various in kind and so delicate in reacting to changes of season and circumstance that, in the budding, colouring, and fading, peculiar to each kind, they exquisitely tell the gradual cycle of the year': thus the Japanese writer Tsuyoshi Tamura. Here we see autumn colour at the monastery of Ryoan-ji in Kyoto.

Is this garden formal, or asymmetrical, or is there a dominant focal point? Traditional Japanese gardens must observe many rules about triangular organization with groups of threes or fives and sevens, informality resulting from elongated triangles.[126] Visitors may merely sense rather than understand these effects. Straight lines and right angles are rare. Such counterpoint precludes any central focus, so that each element signifies only in relation to the others. The sculptor Richard Serra noted in Kyoto that 'the layout of the gardens is based on the perceptual principles of time, meditation and motion. This concept of space is essentially different from our western concept which is based on central

Ronneby Gardens in Sweden illustrate the challenge of adapting sacred Asian traditions to secular Western usage, but the soft natural tones, curvilinear forms, and play of moist, filtered light suit northern Europe as well as Japan.

perspective and arranges all objects on a line emanating from the eye of a static viewer. In the Zen gardens, directions, continuity and paths work together to deny a fixed measure.'[127] Junichiro Tanizaki concurs: 'Beauty is not a substance in its own right but a simple play of shadows, of light and dark produced by the juxtaposition of various substances.'[128]

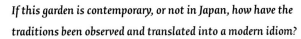

If this garden is contemporary, or not in Japan, how have the traditions been observed and translated into a modern idiom?
The Japanese-American sculptor Isamu Noguchi [*below*] claims that 'the Japanese tradition allows for the greatest latitude'.[129] Western modernists and minimalists appreciate Japanese emphasis on form-defining space, especially asymmetrical formalism. Some, like Noguchi, pursue the abstraction and reduction of natural energies; others, Eastern and Western, extend exploration into theories of chaos and fractal geometry. For the architect Tadao Ando, architecture is 'order abstracted from nature. It is light, sky and water made abstract.'[130] Western ecologists appreciate the Japanese 'osmosis' between humankind and the biosphere, though they reject symbolic miniaturization (especially bonsais). The best Japanese-inspired gardens today explore metaphysical space rather than copying ornamental detail. One stone lantern does not a Japanese garden make, especially when such objects become merely decorative.

BELOW The Isamu Noguchi Sculpture Garden in New York (USA) illustrates this Japanese-American designer's mastery of tradition (the careful placing of natural stones) translated into contemporary arrangements which avoid the single focus and symmetries of Western art.

TWO VIEWS

This is what the Japanese do to perfection. They sit snug under a roof on silky mats with paper screens to deflect the draughts as the rain anoints, then polishes, then seeps into the landscape. Around them aucubas glisten, maples nod and bamboos bow, while the rivulets of rain form into preordained pools in the moss.

Hugh Johnson, British garden writer, 2002[131]

In the West, once Judeo-Christian beliefs replaced ancient ones, man found himself in the centre of the world, chosen by God to dominate and enslave wild nature for his own uses. The image of Paradise thus created, marked by man's authority, was a highly organized, structured garden where nature was tamed, obedient, her bounties and pleasures reserved to those selected to enjoy them for eternity. In the East, man's role in the universe is perceived quite differently: he is merely one among all the elements which compose the world and shares with all the others a fragment of divine being. This sense of unity, globality, can be found in all the philosophic and religious currents which, from India to Japan, have crossed Asia and informed its special sense of nature. Thus eastern landscapes are inspired by wild and remarkable places, real or mystical, regions inhabited by the gods.

Erik Borja, French designer, in *Zen Gardens: Space and Illusion*, 2000

The seventh-floor courtyard of the Marunouchi Hotel in Tokyo was designed in 2002 by the architectural firm of Mitsubishi Jisho Sekkei. Its tree grid and asymmetrical stripes echo both American modernism and Japanese classicism.

In 1939, the modernist designer Shigemori Mirei imagined this contemporary interpretation of the gravel and moss garden for the Tofuku-ji temple in Kyoto. His avowed aim was to create a work of 'timeless modernity'.

Ten Questions for Modernist, Minimalist, and Conceptualist Gardens

We understand avant-garde landscape architecture like architecture and the other arts as
a translation of abstract ideas, ideas of nature, ecology and society.

Peter, Anneliese and Tilman Latz, German garden designers, 2008[132]

The greatest contribution a designer can make is to link the human and the natural in such
a way as to recall our fundamental place in the scheme of things. The design of the landscape
should not be a superficial reordering of natural elements merely to delight the eye.

Dan Kiley, in *Mirrors of Paradise*, 2000[133]

How are geometric forms and patterns used here? It is geometric form which most strongly links modernist design (1920s–70s) to minimalist (beginning 1980s) and now conceptualist (1990s to the present), a genealogy widely affirmed by today's designers.[134] Do patterns work here in three dimensions (perhaps as cubes, pyramids, mounds, cones), or as flat, textured planes (diagonals, spirals, grids)? Are shapes symmetrical in the neoclassical tradition, deliberately off-centre, or perhaps a mix of curves and sharp corners? Are the geometries obvious or gradually revealed? What vantage point(s) do you see them from? Do you walk along them, burrow into them, hover over them? Are photographs of this site often taken from an aeroplane? Is there repetition ('seriality'), a single strong 'gesture',[135] or both? Is detailing kept to a minimum so that 'less is more'[136] – the paring away of inessentials that the American landscape architect Peter Walker calls 'reduction and focus'?

PREVIOUS PAGES
Designers working in modernist and conceptualist contexts think architecturally. They challenge conventional assumptions about natural and built space and our place in it, including the secure feeling of ground level or a horizon line. Indoor and outdoors intermingle in surprising ways. Here work by Hungarian-born Vladimir Sitta in Australia (LEFT) and Juan Grimm in Chile (RIGHT).

The British designer Tony Heywood (who revels in biomorphic shapes), here uses modernist squares and rectangles interlocking with echinocactus in 'The Happening' garden, designed for the Westonbirt Festival of 2002.

Topher Delaney of California (USA) often uses more hardscape than plants, with colourful geometric patterning, as in this roof garden looking onto San Francisco Bay. She is known as a specialist in hospital and therapeutic gardens, a major dimension of social consciousness in design today.

What is the relative importance of constructions and hardscape in this space? Do the built elements impose lines, levels and volumes, defining space in three dimensions as in a giant sculpture? In a private property, is the house central or marginal? Are the gardens its extensions – courtyards, outdoor rooms or roof terraces? Is there a sense of flow between indoor and outdoor spaces? Or perhaps nothing is central, and the 'empty spaces' between are as important as the full volumes? Does each outdoor space have a specific function – parking, eating, sports and recreation? Early modernists insisted on an exact equivalence between form and function, rejecting merely 'decorative' features. Functional logic easily expanded into an ideal of garden design as service: 'gardens for people' (Thomas Church) and 'landscape for living' (Garrett Eckbo).[137] Social consciousness inspired much modern design and continues to nourish much conceptualist work.[138]

**What roles do the ground level and the horizon line play in the overall
picture?** Did the designer(s) reshape the land? Kathryn Gustafson
and partners for example 'mould' each site 'in order to reveal
something about the place, add something new, and blend nature
and invention into a seamless whole'.[139] This usually involves
large-scale public projects [*pp. 24–25*]. 'Modern' houses could be
gravity-defying, half-ensconced, or expansive on ground level.
Thus Le Corbusier found 'damp earth' unhealthy and built sail-like
houses, often on stilts, offering framed views of neutral settings
from rooftop terraces. Frank Lloyd Wright professed on the contrary
that 'no house should ever be put ON a hill . . . it should be OF the
hill, belonging to it, hill and house should live together, each the
happier for the other.' Walter Gropius, in New England, wanted
house and garden to be 'all of a piece', the house taking in 'part of
the surrounding area' with 'tentacles of low walls and trellising'.[140]
Is the horizon line visible? The French landscape architect Michel
Courajoud wrote: 'The horizon, where heaven and earth meet,
is a landscape that leads beyond and frees us from enclosure.'[141]

What role or roles are assigned to plants? Modernists and minimalists often used a very limited plant palette simply to accentuate spatial geometries and provide variations in texture. Hedging of various heights and tones (sometimes disparaged as 'green concrete') reinforced lines and volumes. The New Englander Dan Kiley boasted that 'no contours or rebel trees dilute the purity of formal expression' at the Miller House in Ohio.[142] Scandinavians and Californians more easily include natural irregularities. Thomas Church wrote: 'I learned you can take the wall around the tree – that the tree is more important than the axis.'[143] Church also said, however, that his favorite ground cover was asphalt! The Brazilian plantsman Roberto Burle Marx pioneered in reconciling cubist forms with plantsmanship and ecological sensitivity [*pp. 126–27 and opposite*]. Plants may also assume new functions by helping to purify industrial sites (Latz and Partners at Duisberg, Richard Haag in Seattle). Le Corbusier reputedly had little interest in plants, but nonetheless admired horse-chestnut buds as 'a perfect lesson in foresight, accuracy, eloquence and fantasy in diversity'.[144]

What is the rapport between buildings and their setting?

Le Corbusier's 'box-kite' buildings, wrote Russell Page, were best complemented by 'wild and haphazard growth'[145] – cultural artefact confronting raw nature. Modernists, minimalists and conceptualists all reject a Romantic vision of nature with its 'irrelevant associations with botany, horticulture or nature worship' (Garrett Eckbo), but many also reject the opposition of culture and nature. Links between buildings and 'earth, plants, rocks and water' may affirm Eckbo's ideal 'organic integration of man with nature'.[146] Trees or desert plants, themselves architectural, dialogue with built forms, as when the Californian Isabelle Greene uses graphic plant patterning in subtle greys and greens around minimalist architecture [p. 108]. Marc Nucera in southern France sculpts spontaneous woodland to echo architectural gesture [p. 189].[147] Vegetal roofs offer another successful mix of formal line, textural irregularity and ecological function. The Mexican architect Luis Barragán's pioneer work 'stands at the point where architecture, gardens and sculpture meet and mingle'; his masterpiece village reconstruction among lava fields at El Pedregal is deemed an expression of 'humanistic ecology'.[148]

Are colours and materials here bright or soft, artificial or 'natural', sparse or numerous?

The historian Tim Richardson calls colour 'the strongest visual weapon in the conceptualists' armoury'. Many imitate Luis Barragán whose bright colours highlighted vast flat surfaces, often concrete walls. How is colour here related to texture and how do both catch changing light? Are materials and tones 'natural' (wood, rock) or brashly artificial (chrome, plastic) or both at once ('corten', artificially rusted metal)? Is one colour a central focus or is there reciprocity between several colours? Southern climate designers often celebrate colour (the Brazilian Roberto Burle Marx [pp. 126–27, 188], the French Mediterraneans Arnaud Maurières and Eric Ossart, the Californians Martha Schwartz [p. 187] and Topher Delaney [p. 185]). Parisian landscape architects dismiss colour as merely 'decorative', 'floral' and 'feminine', but the French pioneer Bernard Lassus always defended colourful 'ornamentation' as an essential affirmation of place and identity.[149]

Steve Martino creates soft, flowing connections between contemporary homes and surrounding landscapes, often in the Arizona desert (USA). Successive planes, colour and textural variety in the materials chosen are all-important links, but water also has a place of choice.

What elements change, move, and create dynamic energy in this place? Is anything ephemeral or evolving, or is everything permanently nailed down? Even modernist designers dismissive or fearful of plant growth emphasize time and change. Peter Walker wrote: 'Minimalism has to do with light, weather and the seasons and how they can be read against an artefact.'[150] Some favour artificial light at night in private gardens where owners' entertaining is part of the garden experience (Vladimir Sitta in Australia, Paul Cooper in Britain). Both light and water may provide an extraordinary tool for the exploration of space – physical and sometimes spiritual. Dan Pearson says, 'Water brings the sky down to the earth' [*cf. p. 121*]. Kathryn Gustafson and Herbert Dreiseitl are famous for imaginative uses of water. Festival gardens are temporary by definition and often include wind- or water-powered mobile elements.

Where landscape and growing plants are 'part of the picture' they may be carefully framed as here by the designer Ted Smyth in New Zealand. In such cases, seasonal change and weather patterns will be brought into the heart of the garden experience.

A pool in such a setting – in Chile, designed by Juan Grimm – not only establishes ties between intimate, everyday life and the infinite, it also evokes the whole cycle of water, bringing sky to earth, visually and symbolically.

What happened on this spot before designers intervened, and what is intended for its future? How has the site's history affected the design? Is this place, like so many works by contemporary landscape architects, the memorial of some historic event? Pure modernism, evolving right after World War One, deliberately cut ties with the past, seeking universals.[151] Postmodern work (1970s–80s) exploited historic association for deliberately decorative parody, another way of rejecting the past or mocking its importance. Today, however, 'site memory' has become a basic design tenet all over the world. Often invoked is the 'palimpsest' – a manuscript half erased before being written on once again, where traces of earlier versions can still be seen. There are many imaginative ways of 'making time visible'. The German modernist designer Ludwig Gerns simply painted white and grey the various parts of the 19th-century villa he lives in to indicate different periods of construction.[152]

Festival gardens offer great scope for creative conceptual design – here 'Réflexions colorées' by Hal Ingberg, at the International Garden Festival, Jardins de Métis/Reford Gardens, Quebec (Canada). Coloured glass panels surround a small stand of birch trees.

Can you grasp a guiding concept here, one which perhaps links geometric forms to some spiritual or philosophical dimension?
If so, how is the abstract idea given material expression? Nature, in some idealized form, is usually cited once again. The sculptor Henry Moore followed in the steps of Frank Lloyd Wright when he asserted that 'The whole of nature is an endless demonstration of shape and form.'[153] The American architect George Hargreaves links geometric design to the natural energies of each site. In their Garden of Cosmic Speculation in Scotland, Charles Jencks and Maggie Keswick evoke microbiology and astrophysics [*p. 186*]. If you have trouble relating abstract concepts to the scene before you, consider imagining a change of viewpoint or scale: gardens by Burle Marx or by Isabelle Greene imitate river landscapes seen from an aeroplane [*p. 108*]. Japanese modernism builds on an ancient tradition of metaphoric miniaturization: a single, well-chosen stone symbolizes rather than represents a mountain.

BELOW At the Gardens of the Alchemist and Botanical Garden of Magic Plants in Provence, France, Arnaud Maurières and Eric Ossart contrast esoteric medieval symbolism with popular lore. Squares are graphically outlined in light-catching, ever- changing live willow fencing.

Do you feel welcome? Invited, excluded, overwhelmed, underwhelmed? Is there an explicit attempt to communicate to you a guiding concept? Are you expected to discover it gradually on site (as in a labyrinth), inform yourself beforehand, enjoy the mystery, or take pleasure in just being there, regardless of what the creator(s) had in mind? If you are in a big urban park, does the link between form and function make clear the activities open to you? If there is parody, playfulness or riddles, are they meant for your enjoyment as in Tony Heywood's London parks, or do they remain deliberately hermetic? Tim Richardson concludes: 'Many conceptualist designs contain clues or elements of narrative which are quite deeply buried and must be pointed out to visitors. Indeed, all conceptualist landscape design should ideally work equally well in the context of an "open" interpretation – where the design is not perhaps correctly "read" or understood by users – quite as much as in situations where visitors are actively engaged participants.'[154]

TWO VIEWS

My approach to the earth began as a reaction against geometry. I used to think it an arrogance imposed upon nature, and still do. But I've also realized that it is arrogance to think man invented geometry. As regards my own work, I'd like to think geometry has appeared in it to the same degree I have found it in nature ... Having said all this, I am always suspicious of geometry, cautious in using it. This last year saw my first use of the spiral. It's taken me a long time to come to terms with this form, so evident in nature. I still avoid the overblown spiral. I prefer that of the unfolding fern, which gives the impression of endless growth, or of the simple ammonite in stone.

Andy Goldsworthy, in conversation with John Fowles, 1990[155]

... multiple senses of place or orientations radically stretched, compressed and hybridised between the local and the global, the popular and the academic, the virtual and real, the Euclidean and the fractal, the cultural and the natural – and most pressingly, a place between the indigenous and the exotic. Perhaps all this can be found within the metaphoric scope of the Garden, the core terrain of landscape architecture.

Richard Weller, Australian architecture critic, 2003[156]

José de Yturbe's court at Las Palmas West (Mexico) evokes both Islamic models and the work of his compatriot Luis Barragán. Palm trees have of course an ancient – and modern – symbolism all their own. Their current popularity even in temperate climates attests to its power.

Experts Choose their Favourite Gardens round the Globe

Twenty garden experts were asked to choose three gardens or parks that each would particularly recommend visiting. These could be places deemed important in general garden history or choices important in the expert's own personal development. The garden makers consulted are themselves world travellers, many working on several continents. Some have international reputations as landscape architects specializing in innovative public projects, others provide models for home gardening much appreciated by owners of the smallest plots. Many are prolific garden writers and others are renowned as botanists or horticulturalists. Some are simply owners of gardens which have had considerable public success. All were asked to cite work other than their own and all but two complied. Some are laconic, others expansive, many had trouble sticking to just three! We have left them to speak for themselves, each in his or her own voice. Each selection is a self-portrait.

JOHN BROOKES English designer [p. 120] and writer, who, already in the 1960s, linked gardening to international design trends in architecture and art, while, in his numerous books and courses, creating models for everything from extensive country estates to small urban gardens. See a recent biography by Barbara Simms, *John Brookes: Garden and Landscape Designer* (London 2007).

An iconic garden which influenced me hugely when I was starting out to design, a Thomas Church must – the **Donnell Garden at Sonoma**, California, of 1948. In 1979, we drove out to the garden early one promising day and as the mists rose there was my dream garden, sited on a rocky hillside looking over the Sonoma River which winds its way to the Pacific. The river's twists and turns are reinterpreted into the curves of a sinuous swimming pool, surrounded by a redwood deck. At the time I was heavily into abstract expressionism in painting and Tommy's theory based on cubism, that a garden should have no beginning and no end – it just flowed – really fascinated me, and his shapes have haunted me all my life.

I'm cheating here putting the work of the great Brazilian plantsman/designer Roberto Burle Marx with that of the Mexican architect Luis Barragán. Some years ago I was working on a hotel garden in the mountains outside São Paulo and my client took me to see a 'Roberto' garden which had been converted into a small public park – **Flamengo Park in Rio de Janeiro.** The house had been removed, but the garden was still intact. It's the famous one with a chequerboard of grass – each square divided by metal and the long fountain wall. What makes Roberto so significant is the fact that he started life as an artist, and then became a garden designer using indigenous plant material to superb aesthetic effect. Luis Barragán takes modernist principles another step forward, not only in the styling of his buildings but in their exotic colouring as well: Mies van der Rohe and Mondrian are both present in his inspiration. The seeming sculptural simplicity of his buildings and the spaces between them are epitomized in his famous **San Cristobal Stables outside Mexico City** of 1967–68.

The Bagh-e Shahzadeh, an oasis garden built by the Governor of Kerman at Mahan in Iran.

For sheer knockout spectacle my third garden is in Iran. It's the
Bagh-e Shahzadeh at Mahan, Iran [p. 201], built in the 1890s. The
garden is a jewel within its arid desert setting – a tribute to the use
of water if ever I saw one. Within the high walls of the garden all
is calm. It is in the garden rather than the house that Persian life
was enjoyed, in the shade of trees, with the sound of gentle falling
water between mirror pools, stepping down a long thin site. The
background is of high mountains, from which water was channelled
to be stored and then fed to this lovely place. For me this garden
epitomizes the garden imagery of earlier Islam, for few people
cherished the garden ideal more, in imagination, in language, in
the arts and in their religion. This is not a 'horticultural' garden in
Western terms, rather a sanctuary from external elements created
by the integration of delicate pavilions centred upon a watery axis.
Along its sides and stepping gently down, two waterways are lined
with tall cypress. The sun's glare is reduced to a filigree of light and
shadow. There is little grass, but flowers are scattered about as pots
of colour and fragrance, in deep shade or in patches of filtered sun.

MURIEL DE CUREL Owner with her husband of the Château
de Saint-Jean-de-Beauregard near Paris [p. 88]. Twice a year, a highly
successful plant fair is held there, featuring perennials in April
and vegetables in November.

Kerdalo in Brittany, in France, because it is a garden made by a
painter [Prince Wolkonsky] with extraordinary sensitivity to colour,
a garden that, after visiting it, keeps you dreaming for months on
end, a garden I really love.

Sissinghurst Castle, in Kent, England [*opposite*]. An absolute 'must'
for everyone, a dream garden.

And for the classical tradition, also very important, **Vaux le Vicomte**
[p. 41] represents the best of French classicism in all its purity.
I think that all those châteaux would be nothing without their
gardens to show them off. This one is the best thought out, the
most thoughtful of classical gardens, the perfect type of the great
art of the French 17th century.

The legendary white gardens at Sissinghurst
Castle (Kent, England), begun in 1930 by
Vita Sackville-West. White gardens are still
being made in its image today.

HELEN DILLON Creator of a famous garden near Dublin in Ireland [*p. 139*], intrepid traveller, writer and lecturer.

Great Dixter, Christopher Lloyd's garden in England [*pp. 134, 137*]. Absolutely tops. Great Dixter is a celebration of good gardening, from how-to basics to the high art of putting plants together. It was loved and gardened, thought about and cared for, throughout the lifetime of its owner Christopher Lloyd, who enjoyed discussing plants and plantings with a series of head gardeners (especially Fergus Garrett), friends and visitors. The garden at Great Dixter is a sublime example of perfect balance between good design (by Lutyens) and thrilling plants.

Mount Stewart, County Down, Northern Ireland [*pp. 224–25*].

Dan Hinkley and Robert Jones's new garden, at Indianola, in Washington State, USA. It had only just begun when I saw it, but it's on water. I saw there two parent eagles feeding a chick on a huge nest quite near the house. Dan is a highly renowned plantsman.

The New York Botanical Garden. Gregory Long, the president, is one of my great heroes. This garden is brilliantly run.

Chanticleer, at Wayne, Pennsylvania, near Philadelphia [*opposite*], a top US public garden, very good!

Carmel Duignan's garden, Library Road, Shankhill, County Dublin, Ireland – small, very good plants, but she does love her plants so.

The much-loved Chanticleer Garden near Philadelphia (USA), formerly the estate of Christine and Adolph Rosengarten, Sr, open to the public since 1993.

CALI DOXIADIS Greek writer and gardener, who divides her time between Spain, New York and Corfu [*p. 54*]; former president of the Mediterranean Garden Society.

Ninfa, in Lazio near Rome [*opposite*]. I once said, half-jokingly, that my favourite garden designer was Piranesi. If Piranesi were indeed a garden designer, Ninfa would have been his most representative design. Against the background of sun-baked mountains, a green unfettered garden is laid out among the ivy-clad ruins of a medieval village. It's crossed by a swift creek of cool transparent spring water and artfully disposed conduits that turn this former marsh into an oasis. A perfect combination of art, nature and time.

Heidi Gildemeister's garden on a mountainside in north-eastern Mallorca [*p. 162*]. The most eloquent example I know of a garden that is 'natural' in every way, with the hardscape formed by the wind-sculpted boulders of a rocky slope ending in steep cliffs offering panoramic sea views, with paths meandering through existing openings, and spring water collected in subtly rearranged rocky basins. The softscape, artfully developed around the existing shady native oaks and olive trees, with clipped Mediterranean shrubs and seasonal wild and naturalized bulbs and annuals, stays green without irrigation throughout the summer in this hot and arid area.

The 'avli' – a typical Greek garden that is nowhere and everywhere, the inevitable creation of a land- and water-poor population. Set out over a few square metres adjoining or surrounded by a house, within reach of carried water, it is partially paved, with the paved area shaded by a grapevine pergola creating a summer dining area adorned with recycled whitewashed tins containing flowering plants (typically stocks and roses) and herbs such as spearmint and basil. Crowded into the open area are several fruit trees – lemon and orange, Japanese medlar or apricot. They are underplanted with a succession of seasonal vegetables – perennials such as artichokes and broad beans as well as the summer annual ones, interspersed with marigolds.

The gardens of Ninfa, near Rome, lie among the ruins of a medieval town excavated by the Caetani family, on an ancient Roman site.

HENK GERRITSEN Artist and garden designer, owner of
Priona in the Netherlands [*pp. 64, 65*], colleague and author with
Piet Oudolf of *Planting the Natural Garden*, *Gardening with Grasses*,
and *Dream Plants for the Natural Garden*.

A difficult question, because generally I don't think much of other
gardens. I find them either too tidy and controlled or too wild,
lacking design. The three gardens that have inspired me most are:

The garden of Kasteel Baexem – Baexem Castle – in the south of
Holland. Very little known, but open to the public. An absolutely
ravishing garden full of follies and surprises, and with a fantastic
atmosphere. www.kasteel-baexem.nl

De Heliant, the nursery of Heilien Tonckens in the north-east of
Holland, which is actually more of a garden. The most beautiful
wildflower garden that I know of. www.deheliant.nl

I would have chosen Mark Brown's garden at Varengeville in
France, but that will close down soon. He is currently making
a new garden nearby, which will be as good, I'm sure, but it will
take many years to establish. So instead I will mention the
Manoir d'Eyrignac in the Dordogne [*left*]. It may surprise you that
I select a formal garden, but I find it breathtaking, because unlike
any other formal garden it fits perfectly into the surrounding
countryside.

The Manoir d'Eyrignac in the Dordogne
(France) has belonged to the same family
for five hundred years, but these formal
shapes were created in the 1960s.

HEIDI GILDEMEISTER Owner of an iconic garden in Mallorca [*pp. 2, 162*], author of *Mediterranean Gardening* and *Gardening the Mediterranean Way: Practical Solutions for Summer-Dry Climates*, winner of the Best Garden in Spain award for the year 2000.

The Botanical Garden of Soller, Mallorca [*right*]. It specializes in the island's own native plants and shows to perfection how and where to plant these in order to make the planting succeed. Surrounded by mountains and orange groves, the setting is lovely. And they are set up for visitors.

Charles Shoup's vanished garden in the Peloponnese. Although it cannot be visited any more, accounts and photographs in several books give us an idea of its former glory. The sensitivity with which Charles had created this garden from zero, suited to the countryside, to the past of the land, was memorable.

Kirstenbosch Botanic Garden near Cape Town, South Africa [*p. 76*]. The concept is somewhat similar to Soller's, but the scale is quite different. Here the visitor sees on something like 400 hectares (1000 acres) the Cape Province's own flora – only that, unmixed with plants from other regions. And the birds that come to drink nectar from these flowers (and do the fertilizing) are lovely. Best to set several days aside for such an unforgettable visit.

These gardens impressed me by their logic, the consequence and knowledge with which they were carried out once the theme had been decided upon, the delight they gave – not to forget the information . . .

The beautiful Botanical Garden of Soller in Mallorca houses an institute committed to conserving the endemic, rare and endangered plant species of the Balearics.

ISABELLE GREENE Californian designer [*p. 108*], currently working on five acres of park-like grounds around the Santa Barbara Museum of Natural History to purify and infiltrate the runoff; and also on the restoration of the garden of one of the best of the famous Greene and Greene houses (for her, a family connection!) in Pasadena.

I'm going to limit my recommendations to gardens that to me were done with a great deal of heart (not vast gardens for display of fortune or power or space).

Fletcher Steele's **Naumkeag, at Stockbridge**, Massachusetts, USA [*opposite*], has a lot of curious innovative responses to the site and the family. He was quite courageous in his day to be so whimsical and kind of 'non sequitur'.

Burle Marx's wonderful, rambunctious **Monteiro Garden in Rio de Janeiro**, even though that is a large garden. To me it has Burle Marx's vigorous, colourful, lovable personality all over. He must have spent most of his time there for at least a couple of years. It shows great devotion to art for the earth.

The other person who comes to mind is A. E. Bye, an American designer, whose designs are so subtle you really don't know that something has been done. Largely he dealt with very subtle gradations of land forms. There is particularly stunning photography of one of his sites with snow, melted in places. It all seems natural but is too natural to be really natural, very underplayed. He does something to give the land a voice but holds himself back, his own ego is not very much there, he makes the land speak. [Public works by A. E. Bye include gardens for the Harvey Hubbell Corporation in Orange, Connecticut, the Jefferson Memorial park in Washington, and the pocket park at 77 Water Street in Manhattan.]

Two others . . .

Dumbarton Oaks, in Washington, D.C., by Beatrice Ferrand: in spite of meeting very traditional expectations for 'axes' and 'focal

The much-photographed Blue Steps of the American architect Fletcher Steele on the Naumkeag Estate, at Stockbridge, Massachusetts (USA), were built in 1938.

points', working with the same family over a period of years, she managed to introduce a lot of whimsy.

And last but not least is Richard Haag's **Gas Works Park in Seattle**, Washington, also in the USA, which is really funny. I visited in a snowstorm, it was a magical experience.

KATHRYN GUSTAFSON American landscape architect, who trained and began her career in France; now based in Britain and the US (Gustafson Porter in London and Gustafson Guthrie Nichol in Seattle). Among her many works are the Diana, Princess of Wales, memorial fountain in Hyde Park and the Crystal Palace Park in London, the National Botanic Gardens in Wales, public parks in Chicago [pp. 24–25], Amsterdam, Beirut and Singapore, and 'Fragments of Garden History' ('Les Jardins de l'Imaginaire') in Terrasson, France.

Versailles [p. 40]: I go three or four times a year, I learn every time I go, today around the Lac des Suisses. I haven't done it for about ten years, just the sheer scale of it! Le Nôtre's vision is so fantastic! And from there at the very far end, you look back and you see the Hundred Steps on either side of the Orangerie, and you sense the scale as you never do unless you pull way back. You have to walk to the other end of the Lac des Suisses to get it all in context. That was great. And then when you get to the far end, you find the Sun King on his horse. And just as I came up to the statue, there were two trains right behind him, elevated some ten meters above his head, in the background! There is a series of trees, then one of those old elevated train tracks that are like on vaults? You can't see any of the brick structure because it's covered with ivy, so you don't expect this modern blue and white train to go whizzing past his head! Versailles handles formality and intimacy at the same time: you can get lost in all these little secret holes or you can do the grand act, so many scales, such brilliance . . .

Filoli, in northern California, USA [*opposite*]. Still a great garden to go to, wonderful! It's a series of rooms, it's a procession of things. Not grand landscaping like Versailles, no way, but a series of very well articulated rooms that contain, in a way, the whole history of gardens. There's a knot garden in there that's one of the most beautiful in the world.

One aspect of the richly diverse Filoli Garden near San Francisco, California (USA), originally designed for the Bourn family in the early 20th century.

The other one I absolutely love is **Schönbrunn in Vienna**, Austria, that huge garden with all the terraces and the hedging, the super narrow hedges. I love the whole composition of it.

RICHARD HAAG, famous American landscape architect based in Seattle, creator of the iconic Gas Works Park and the Bloedel Reserve gardens [p. 122].

Saiho-ji [Koke Dera], Kyoto, Japan. Calmly move toward selflessness into a shadowed mosaic of moss [p. 172]. Buddha is in the concept, his disciples rest in the details.

The Woodland Cemetery, Stockholm, Sweden [pp. 218–19]. All the landscape elements interplaying in complementing contrast: closure/opening; prospect/refuge; the earth – dug/piled, leveled/folded; woodland/prairie; water – playful/ponded; movement – symmetrical/occult; diorama – pagan/Christian.

Vietnam Memorial, Washington, D.C. [below]. The gravity of the collective sorrow mounts as the procession descends. The names of the dead distort the reflections of the living.

The eloquent Vietnam Memorial in Washington, D.C. (USA), designed by Maya Ying Lin, 1982.

The historic gardens of the Villa Cetinale near Siena (Italy) combine the best of two great gardening traditions, 17th-century Italian and 20th-century English.

PENELOPE HOBHOUSE Perhaps the world's most famous gardener, historian, and garden writer in English. Her books include *Colour in Your Garden, Plants in Garden History, Penelope Hobhouse on Gardening, Penelope Hobhouse's Garden Designs,* and *Penelope Hobhouse's Natural Planting.* She was for many years in charge of the National Trust property Tintinhull House in Somerset. She has designed gardens all over the world, including 'The Country Garden' for the Royal Horticultural Society at Wisley in Surrey.

My favourite gardens all combine a framework with imaginative planting. Each one is also perfect for its setting.

Villa Cetinale near Siena, in Italy [*above*], which combines history with perfect setting in oak woods full of wild flowers. Formal 17th-century design by the Chigi family restored with loving care and much enhanced by the late Lord Lambton. Includes an English Flower Garden originally laid out by an Edwardian English Chigi grandmother.

Stourhead in Wiltshire, created by Henry Hoare between 1745 and 1770. Almost the first English landscape park with allegorical temples, grotto, etc., round a lake – enhanced in the mid-19th century with newly introduced dark conifers from the Pacific north-west. The circuit walk is planned for a series of surprises as follies come into view. Perfect to visit in winter.

Helen Dillon's garden in Dublin, Ireland [p. 139], combines talented design with plantmanship. Helen is an extraordinarily gifted gardener and with frequent changes keeps the garden dynamic. I admire it and her without reservation.

LAND-I A group of landscape architects, formed of Marco Antonini, Roberto Capecci and Raffaella Sini. They have participated extensively in international competitions in Europe and North America and created one of the most successful projects at the International Garden Festival of Chaumont in France.

The Tarot Garden, Capalbio, Tuscany, Italy. Niki de Saint Phalle's esoteric creation is a garden that appeals to people of all ages and on many levels. It is a tribute to Gaudí's work, influenced by the surreal sculptures of the 'Sacro Bosco' of Bomarzo, and the most personal, almost biographic work imaginable. But more than all of these references, when visiting it, one starts a journey through a series of spaces where ideals, site, vegetation and work of art resonate magically.

The Woodland Cemetery – Skogskyrkogården – in Stockholm, Sweden [*left*]. Three quarries of gravel, surrounded by a forest of over 100 hectares (some 250 acres) where memory shapes the landscape. The remembrance is not submitted to single graves, codified objects disposed by the pity of the grievers, but to the forms and scale of the site, to the shape of its profile between earth and sky, to the transit between wood and lawn, to the dialogue between shade and light.

Stourhead, Wiltshire, England. You will need to visit Stourhead on a misty, rainy, autumn day. It will appear naked, bare, the garden buildings floating on the 'nature improved' hillside, silently disposed following a precise geometry. A path connects them, telling a story that becomes unique to the visitor's soul, evoking images of past glories, of forgotten poems. Some gardens are 'such stuff as dreams are made on', but it seems its life will never be completed with a 'sleep'.

The Woodland Cemetery, Stockholm
(Sweden), designed by Gunnar Asplund
and Sigurd Lewerentz. The Crematorium,
by Asplund, dates from 1939.

LATZ AND PARTNERS – the German landscape architects
Peter Latz, his wife Anneliese and their son Tilman – have created
dozens of innovative parks and gardens all over the world, from
small private domains to major public projects [p.27].

Peter and Anneliese suggest three gardens which have had 'great
influence on our planning philosophy and which of course we
would also recommend to visit', the first two experienced when
'very young'.

The Garden of Gethsemane at the foot of the
Mount of Olives, in East Jerusalem (Israel).

The garden of the Castello Ruspoli in Vignanello, Italy. Visiting Italian Renaissance gardens nearly forty years ago, we stood on the balcony of the Castello Ruspoli together with the white-haired gardener. He told us that, when he had finished clipping the last medallion of the parterre, he used to stand at the far end at the balustrade, to look into the peaceful pastoral landscape, then turn round, to walk slowly to the direction of the castle and to begin again – clipping his sovereign's initials into the first hedges. Year after year, decade after decade, being completely even with himself. Ever since we had a dream, and many years later we tried to create our homage to Vignanello in our own garden – perhaps typical for a European in the north of the Alps – to create a vital Mediterranean consciousness, a Mediterranean way of life by means of design.

The gardens of Hadrian's Villa, Tivoli, near Rome, Italy. The same journey brought us to the Villa Adriana. We never thought that ruins could be so impressive: the Poikile with its large dimensions, the beautiful Canopus mirroring the Caryatids in its green water, and all the other building structures and garden spaces emit an incredible peacefulness and generosity. They had a lasting influence on our later professional thinking and acting.

The Garden of Gethsemane in Jerusalem, Israel [*left*]. For us, this is the garden absolute, existing already for more than two thousand years and continuing to exist on and on with the same plants: olive trees, their mighty trunks scarred and hollow, but still with shady evergreen canopies.

Tilman has three parks and gardens in mind when speaking of influence: the *Jardin du Luxembourg in Paris*, the landscape garden of *Rousham House* in the UK – these two are absolute favourites – and also *Hadrian's Villa*.

ARNAUD MAURIÈRES and **ERIC OSSART** Leading French designers of city parks, country gardens and many elegant Mediterranean gardens in Europe and North Africa [*pp. 66, 194–95*]. Authors also of several excellent garden books – *Paradise Gardens: Landscape Gardening in the Islamic Tradition* and *L'Art de vivre dehors: Les jardins de Ossart et Maurières*.

The places which have moved us the most are the following, in order of discovery:

The Paul Maymou nursery in Bayonne, in southern France, created by his father and now run by his daughter. The father had planted many trees from Japan (maples, dogwoods, etc.). This was not fashionable around 1900 but the plants are now trees and the nursery rows have become a forest. The spontaneity of this garden is really magic, all the more so because the original landscape with its vales and marshes contributes to the mood. We feel as if we were in a Kurosawa film when we walk in that garden.

The house of Luis Barragán in Mexico City, because we would not be the designers that we are without Barragán. We could go on and on about this but the most important thing is his reconciliation between architecture and garden. Not vernacular architecture which is spontaneously integrated into natural settings, but a sophisticated, urban style in osmosis with the outdoors, vegetation, sky and water. Today that property is listed as a UNESCO World Heritage site.

The Azem Palace, Hama, Syria. To enter the courtyard of the Azem Palace is to enter a myth. Here was the source of all Arab gardens, of the *Romance of the Rose*, the *Romance of Alexander*, pillars of Europe's medieval literature. This same source fed the imaginations of the Western world's first gardeners. We have over and over again invented such places before discovering their underlying reality: a perfect harmony between stone, water, shade, light and trees.

The Azem Palace in Hama (Syria), a strong example of Ottoman design, was the first residence of governor Assad Pasha Al Azem before he was transferred to Damascus in 1743. The tree is a giant magnolia. Beyond it is an octagonal fountain.

SANDY OVENSTONE Owner-gardener of famous historic and contemporary gardens at Stellenberg in Cape Town, South Africa, well-known plantswoman, and veteran garden visitor.

Hidcote Manor in England for the brilliance of classical design, vision and plantings and a garden of different rooms [*above*].

Le Prieuré d'Orsan, in the Berry region of France [*p. 15*], for a spiritual and moving experience through green structure which elevates you to being in a living cathedral, created by two architects with dedication.

Sasnières, a garden in the Loire valley in France, created by the owner and run and worked in by the family. It is set in a village with beautiful vistas, and is a true plantman's garden.

ABOVE The stilt garden at Hidcote Manor in Gloucestershire, England. Made by Major Lawrence Johnston in the early 20th century, this is perhaps Britain's most influential modern garden.

GIUPPI PIETROMARCHI Countess Pietromarchi is the owner of La Ferriera, one of Tuscany's most famous private gardens (at Capalbio), and author of a book on the gardens of Ninfa.

Mount Stewart in Ireland [*below*] for the extravance of expressing with plants many passages of the owner's life, full of imagination.

Ninfa [*p. 207*], in Italy near Rome, the most romantic and nostalgic garden, where secret sentiments are expressed with plants and blooming roses.

Third . . . If I had to leave and go to a desert island I would certainly take with me *my own garden*, where I spent passion, work, disappointment, crisis and love, more love than any creature can ever give me!

BELOW The gardens of Mount Stewart House in County Down, Northern Ireland, created in the 1920s by Edith, Lady Londonderry.

ELIZABETH SCHOLZ Distinguished internationally known botanist, born in South Africa; emeritus director of the Brooklyn Botanic Garden International Tour Office, and highly appreciated guide for decades on the BBG's garden trips.

Kirstenbosch [p. 76]. Named Africa's most beautiful garden, it is indeed so. The backdrop of the eastern slopes of Table Mountain provides 'borrowed scenery' to set off the floral wonders of Kirstenbosch, which features South African native plants. The garden's sheltered location and Mediterranean-type climate ensure something of interest year round. A further unique feature is the natural forest which surrounds the garden and attracts plentiful bird life.

Les Quatre Vents [*opposite*]. North America's most remarkable private garden, in Canada, has vistas of mountains, woods and fields, a complex of hedges forming garden 'rooms', and water used to great effect, especially in reflecting pools (some with swans). A number of garden styles are featured, also architectural elements such as a hexagonal music pavilion, a Lutyens arch, a Chinese Moon Bridge, a Japanese Tea House, all in appropriate settings. For the adventurous there are rope bridges, and for all whimsical frog musicians.

Shisendo, Kyoto, Japan [p. 166]. In a city of many famous gardens, Shisendo is a surprise; attached to a villa dedicated to famous poets, this intimate Kyoto garden is approached through a small rustic gate and viewed from a veranda. Azalea bushes sheared into rounded shapes have pink flowers in spring, but are a restful green at other times. The ground is raked white sand. Beyond is a hillside of trees. Many maples provide brilliant color in autumn.

The Water Course in Les Jardins de Quatre Vents, at La Malbaie in Quebec (Canada). It was designed by its owner, Francis H. Cabot, and, although very recent, has already attracted attention worldwide.

FUMIAKI TAKANO Japanese landscape architect, working all over Asia and in the West, with ecological concerns, and also parks for children.

Japanese Gardens of the Jardin Albert Kahn, in a suburb of Paris. The Jardin Albert Kahn was created by the French philanthropist between 1895 and 1910. Mr Takano was, at the time, part of a design community known as Team Zoo, 'commissioned to create gardens of Japanese inspiration here in 1988, in which variations of texture and colour created formal echoes of the life of the garden's creator. This was a chance to make a garden in a contemporary Japanese idiom. We tried to symbolize Mr Albert Kahn's life using water.'

Tokachi Millennium Forest (Haobi, Shimizu-cho) in Hokkaido, Japan. A garden with nature, acting as an invitation to the natural environment for people from the city. The project is a collaboration with Mr Dan Pearson, an English garden designer: West meets East.

Japanese Garden in Portland, Oregon, USA, by Professor Takuma Tono [*below*]. Fine traditional Japanese garden, one of the most authentic creations outside Japan.

BELOW The Japanese Garden in Portland, Oregon (USA), was designed by Takuma Tono in the 1960s. This is the dry Zen garden; but Buddhist and Shintoist influences are also present.

ABOVE In the great baroque gardens of Herrenhausen in Hanover (Germany) the 'Golden Figures' stand on the stage of the Garden Theatre, built around 1690.

J. R. P. VAN HOEY SMITH Founder of the International Dendrology Society and ex-director of the famous Trompenburg Arboretum in Rotterdam, The Netherlands.

Herrenhausen [*above*] and *Berggarten*, near each other, in Hanover, Germany. Herrenhausen is fantastically kept in the old French rectangular style, while the Berggarten is a real arboretum with many rare and old specimen trees and shrubs.

Gimborn Arboretum/Pinetum at Doorn. This is the largest Dutch arboretum, with many rare conifers, especially the big and old *Tsugas* and *Sciadopitys* groups. Many cultivars of conifers originate from the Gimborn estate and some have the cultivar name 'Gimbornii'.

Kirstenbosch, Cape Town [*p. 76*]. Here you see practically all South African plants, but the new succulent greenhouse and the big collection of cycads are especially worth visiting. The layout, with Table Mountain in the background, is magnificent.

MADE WIJAYA Leading Asian landscape gardener, author of *Tropical Garden Design, At Home in Bali, The Architecture of Bali*, and *Modern Tropical Garden Design*.

Garden-tomb of the emperor Tu Duc, outside Hué Central, in Vietnam [*above*]. One of the wonders of the tropical world. A series of gardens and royal courtyards created in a forest over several decades. The courtyard walls of the inner sanctum are extraordinary (mossy, handsome but with accents of smashed tiles like a Gaudian palace). The floating pavilions on the lake, the emperor's private quarters and the quarters of the courtyard guards are all exquisitely designed and built. Bonsai-ed trees and potted plants – cycads, adenum and multi-hued euphorbia – dot the courts on 'very Vietnamese' ceramic and stone pedestals. It is from here, and from the neighbouring Hindu province of 'Champa', that the *Plumeria obtusa* probably got its name, 'Temple tree' (called 'champa' in India).

The garden-tomb of the Vietnamese emperor Tu Duc, outside Hué Central. The emperor built this park compound to house an auxiliary palace where he spent much time. After his death in 1883, he was buried here.

Bogor Botanical Gardens, West Java. For tropical colonial botanical splendour you can't beat the Taman Raya (botanical garden) of Bogor, in the hills outside Jakarta, Indonesia. They have the ex-palace of the last Governor General of the Dutch East Indies in one corner, Sir Stamford Raffles' wife's neoclassical rotunda tomb in a bamboo grove at the centre, and giant ponds of the Victoria regina waterlily everywhere. The vast park is crisscrossed with tropical fruit tree avenues, and rills and a raging river run through from the highlands of the volcano Gunung Gede to the south. As at Kew, one can get lost (unlike its possible rivals in Sri Lanka and Mauritius) and one can discover many enchanting, 'forgotten' corners. Spotted deer graze under Java's largest banyan tree in the park outside the old palace.

Kyoto, Japan [*pp. 166, 168–72, 174, 176, 177, 180*]. Being in Kyoto – walking the ancient streets, public gardens, palaces, ryokan, monasteries and shrines – is being in a state of constant garden design euphoria. One feels horticulturally heightened. The garden designers of Kyoto – even the amateurs in the tiny front courtyards of city cafés – teach us everything we need to know about tasty yet sublime hardscape, accent plants in mossy reaches, reflections in water gardens, lanterns as art, indoor–outdoor space (and how best to appreciate a garden from a covered space), pergolas, statuary, and how to be bold with blossoms. Even the herbaceous borders around the ubiquitous vending machines seem artistic. I could name favourite gardens, but, really, one should try to see them all: Kyoto is just one big urban and ancient garden.

I'd also like to mention every country garden I've ever been to in England, as well as the Chelsea Physic Garden in London and Kew [*pp. 82–83*]; in France the châteaux of Fontainebleau, Chenonceau, Chantilly, Villandry [*p. 52*] and Courance; in Spain Cordoba, the Generalife [*p. 46*] and Alhambra in Granada, and Seville; every Wirtz garden in Belgium; Burle Marx's Sítio outside Rio de Janeiro in Brazil [*pp. 126–27*]; in Sri Lanka the Perdinia Botanical Garden in Kandy; in India Humayun's Tomb in Delhi and the Taj West End Hotel Garden in Bangalore; in Java Taman Sari in Jogyakarta and Taman Narmada in West Lombok; the tomb complex of Hafez Mohammad in Shiraz, Iran;

in Hawaii the Allerton Garden, Kuai; in Australia Kings Park, Perth, and the botanical gardens in Sydney, Brisbane and Melbourne; Irish Banochies Garden in Bathsheba, Barbados; in California, USA, the Huntington Gardens in San Marino [*pp. 80–81*], Lotusland in Santa Barbara [*p. 73*], and the Simon Schuller Museum in Pasadena; the Museo Antropológico, Mexico City; in Mauritius, the Botanical Garden and the Oberoi; in Italy Ninfa outside Rome (my all-time favourite) [*p. 207*], the gardens of the Villa d'Este at Tivoli [*pp. 42, 43*], and pocket gardens in Venice; in Portugal Cintra; in Morocco the Al Said Tomb and Majorelle Garden in Marrakech; and in Nepal Kathmandu and the Durbar Square in Baktapur.

PETER WIRTZ Belgian designer, who with his famous father Jacques and brother Martin has created numerous celebrated European gardens [*cf. pp. 51, 112*].

Villa Lante, Bagnaia, Italy [*right, and p. 41*]. The progression from the fine tailored formal garden at the bottom, in dialogue with the cityscape, towards the looser formal composition at the top of the hill, where the old wood reigns, is a master move! Also the water as binding theme, richly executed, is of delightful quality.

Fountain Plaza, Dallas, Texas, USA. The uplifting experience of being taken away from the city nuisances into an unreal world of water and foliage, a true oasis in the middle of the city, is an unforgettable experience. The glass building, sitting in the water with its sunken café where the water is at eye level, the reflection, the powerful Texas light, the excellent tree choice, the virtuous treatment of the complex grading along the adjacent streets, all work together in a powerful statement!

Sissinghurst, Kent, England [*p. 202*]. A remarkable combination of strong architecture in the garden of excellent proportions, with an exuberant planting programme! The high walls covered with clematis and roses, the superb white and yellow gardens, the human scale of the spaces, the impeccable lawns, the beautiful rolling agricultural landscape around: a uniquely balanced and harmonious reference.

The Villa Lante at Bagnaia is perhaps Italy's most admired Renaissance garden. It water effects were invented by Pirro Ligorio, also active at the Villa d'Este [*pp. 42, 43*].

Advice from the Wise

WHAT TO BRING ALONG

A notebook

'The secret of getting more out of a garden visit than an "oo-er, isn't it lovely" experience is to go round at least twice. I go round the first time to enjoy myself and to get an overall idea of the garden, and the second time I take a lot of notes and make crude sketches, because unless you have a marvellous visual memory you forget what you have seen.'

Anne Scott-James, British garden historian[1]

'First, equip yourself with a notebook having waterproof covers . . . write in it your name and address and a plea to the finder to return it to its owner who will pay generous compensation . . . looking through its entries will hold you in good stead as a mind-jogger for years to come. Furthermore there is nothing more encouraging to a garden owner nor more likely to start him or her conversing with you than to see, as a note book clearly demonstrates, that you're serious about your subject.'

Christopher Lloyd, writer and owner of Great Dixter, England[2]

'I remember being with Christopher Lloyd once when he was very cantankerous. Some woman kept asking him the names of plants, he looked at her and he said "Madame, you are not writing this down, you will NOT remember it, you are wasting my time and yours," and turned on his heel . . . I take a notebook everywhere anyway but especially in gardens.'

Lynden Miller, New York garden designer

A sketchpad?

'Drawing trees carefully is a special and rewarding way of learning them. . . . In this way you will fast acquire a kind of tree-love if, as I think, "love" is that kind of knowledge that is deeper than the superficial information accumulated by the everyday functioning of the brain alone.'

Russell Page, English landscape architect[3]

A camera?

Why bring a camera?
Looking through a lens can help you see things about a garden you hadn't noticed with the naked eye, by the very act of framing.

With a camera you can record the experience for later recall, including details you might not have noticed at the time.

'Take pictures also of things you DON'T like so you can figure out why.'

Lynden Miller, New York garden designer

(But always ask permission of the owner before taking pictures!)

Why leave the camera at home?
It can cut you off from the garden experience – and from the owner. The Spanish designer Fernando Caruncho refuses to show his garden to anyone taking pictures, as it keeps interrupting the conversation. He feels also that the camera stresses only the visual qualities of a visit which should engage all the senses, including the sixth, seventh, eighth, ninth . . .

Cameras can become addictive. The French garden photographer Georges Lévêque admits: 'When I visit a new garden, I see it through my viewer which gives me square images. My eye is now trained to see that way, even without my camera!'

'Take time to sit (if the garden is worth it). Make notes to cover your photographs – and ask yourself, why are you snapping away? Enjoy.'

John Brookes, English garden designer

WHO TO VISIT WITH

A friend? The owner?

'…a companion with whom to discuss what you're seeing (and to have a few jokes with) … If the garden owner is with you that complicates matters in some ways. Perhaps your companion can take the pictures and notes while you concentrate on talking and looking. The owner's presence provides insights which often entirely alter your own perceptions.'

Christopher Lloyd, writer and owner of Great Dixter, England[4]

'I saw a Roberto Burle Marx garden in São Paulo once too, but had no one to talk to about it. I enjoy analysing what I'm seeing but I need someone informed to do it with.'

John Brookes, English garden designer

'…a sounding board is indispensable, someone to bounce ideas around with. What do you think of this? How do you feel about these colours? What strikes you about these plants? That sort of analysis helps to garner information that acts as a springboard for other ideas, but be careful, a garrulous companion can be a distinct distraction to observant contemplation and thoughtful serenity.'

Trevor Nottle, writer, Australia[5]

A whole group?

Group visits are often the only way to see exclusive private gardens. They need not be big coach tours pouring in and pouring out of famous sites, the sort that Samuel Johnson already disparaged in 1774 as 'travelling fools and starers'. Today, for many visitors and owners alike, the ideal is small, specialized groups which allow personal dialogue. Pierre and Monique Cuche, who show their experimental Mediterranean garden in southern France by appointment only, appreciate groups of six or seven. Then, they say, 'the most enthusiastic and more knowledgeable people stimulate the others'. The French designers Arnaud Maurières and Eric Ossart, who have often met the public in their gardens, agree: 'Small groups led by sensitive and competent guides are tops; big noisy coachloads are the bottom.' Groups can form in surprising ways. In San Francisco, some garden lovers wanted to visit the famous park at Lotusland in Santa Barbara [p. 73], but were told they could only come as a constituted and labelled group. They decided to called themselves the 'Hortosexuals' – those for whom gardens count more than anything else in life! They have continued to visit under this name ever since.

'Obviously if you are obliged to keep up with a group, and may very likely be "doing" four or five gardens (Heaven forbid more) … there comes a necessary steeling of the will and a determined focus on getting the most out of what could be a once-in-a-lifetime opportunity. Some reading will help here, so do some homework if you can before you begin to travel, and badger the guide for tour notes too, so you can read up on what is in store. Be prepared for the bare fact that some gardens will just be pleasant viewing; this is just as well as you are probably on holiday and may enjoy the relaxation a green and flowery interlude will allow. And be ready for the one or two that you have decided may have something for your scrapbook. In some gardens, tour groups are severely herded about by strict guides with all the skills of a sheep-dog mustering a wayward flock; it may be impossible to escape, but give it a try unless the Polizza are likely to be summoned to attend to any breakaways. A toilet stop may provide an opportunity to study more closely the things you want to see rather than hearing about the glories of the Rococo aviaries, now seriously in advanced decay. However, be sure not to miss the bus!'

Trevor Nottle, writer, Australia[6]

TIMING

Best time of day?

The best hours for visiting depend on the local climate and season. In temperate climates, professional photographers always aim for early morning or late afternoon. In Northern Europe, moist, horizontal light produces long shadows, intensifies colours, brings up surface detailing and makes distant hills recede. Near the Mediterranean, midday is for 'mad dogs and Englishmen' but long mornings and evenings can be golden. But in coastal 'Mediterranean climate' zones, like southern California, midday is best even in summer, because later in the afternoon fog rolls in from the Pacific. Closer to the Equator, where light is vertical, dry sun sharpens focus and brings distant objects closer. Always enquire about local conditions – right after you ask the owners about their own preference for the time of your visit! Many owners favour visits throughout the day to ease pressure, but some insist on opening only when the light is at its most flattering.

Best season?

This is not always what one thinks. Beth Chatto, creator of one of Britain's most famous gardens [*p. 159*], wrote: 'It is a pity, I think, that many garden visitors give up the habit of visiting by the end of September. Many do so sooner, as holidays are over and children back at school. But gardens can give pleasure (and ideas) right into winter. Of course it takes time, years, to create the bones of a garden which will look good when the flowers have gone.'[7] John Brookes says of his visitors at Denmans: 'The wise ones often say "it must be lovely in the winter" – and even come then.' Jean-Paul Dumas, long in charge of the much-visited Jardins de l'Imaginaire in the Dordogne, observes that different kinds of visitors favour different times of year: 'Those who come in the spring or autumn have time, take time. They walk around for enjoyment, out of curiosity. Whereas people who come in August have a gruelling timetable, with only so much time for each visit and no more. They come like consumers intent on buying rather than people really visiting a garden'.

How long should a visit take, and how many gardens can be visited in one day?

Experienced visitors recommend not more than two or three visits per day. Greedy people get into trouble and cause disappointments, not only their own. Once on the French Riviera, the guide of a long overdue group phoned to announce that her charges would not be coming, as they were 'too happy where they were'. For some time afterwards, other requests to visit that garden were not at all well received . . . In planning two or three gardens in a day, be sure also that they are neither too similar in character nor too far apart.

ENJOYING THE GARDEN

'Ask what was there before. When you are walking around, don't forget to turn around and look back in the direction you came from.'

George and Marilyn Brumder, garden owners and visitors, Pasadena, USA

'When you visit a garden, take away only pictures, and leave behind only footprints.'

Merryl Johnson, Country Farm Nursery, near Melbourne, Australia

'Be indulgent, think of what you yourself might have been able or not able to do in that garden.'

Alain Andrio, Riviera gardener, France

'Ask the owners where they like to sit at the end of the day. What they themselves like best or would most like to change in their garden. How much time they spend there and if they work in it themselves.'

Mary Dorra, garden writer, Santa Barbara, Caifornia, USA

'Let yourself be drawn into the place, inspired by it to live outside of time, all your senses aware, looking, feeling, listening, discovering. Don't arrive with a preconceived idea of the garden or of gardens in general. Be curious and greedy for impression, let your eyes move from microscopic to macroscopic, try to understand what the owners are doing and why. Why did they put that bench THERE! If possible, talk to the gardeners.'

Thierry and Monique Dronet,
owners of Berchigranges garden, France

'Try to guess what have been the influences, feelings, dreams of the person who made this garden, what curiosity about the life of plants may have moved him or her, discover what surprises are in store for you, all that is best in the garden maker . . .'

Simone Kroll, Franco-Belgian garden architect

'I like to return to an honest garden that is what it is and does not pretend to be something else. Good backbone, taste and plantsmanship, happy plants and harmony: happy gardeners too. Do I ask too much? Yet there may be nothing of all this and I still would like to return, bewitched or charmed by the owners.'

Heidi Gildemeister, gardener and writer, Mallorca, Spain

'I love gardens that tell their story well. That means that usually there is a theme, and it is well developed. The theme might be native plants, or Buddhist philosophies, or art and nature, or even monocultures of lilacs, tulips, or roses. How well established the theme is (over years of intelligent design and hard work) and how well it is maintained (either through paid staff or devoted volunteers) usually defines the success of the garden for me. I also prefer gardens that use minimal chemicals or are altogether organic because I like the messy, breathing, unpredictable aspect of nature. I don't like gardens that mimic indoor spaces, that are too tidy, and which must be maintained with lots of harmful chemicals.

Gardening with pesticides, herbicides, and synthetic fertilizers seems self-defeating to me; we want nature to thrive, not suffer, through our manipulations.'

Christine Colasurdo, nature writer and gardener, Oregon, USA

'Before leaving, I like to have another look, alone, at the parts of the garden that most aroused my interest and if possible, I like to speak with the maker of the garden. This isn't always possible and it doesn't always work out, but it can be a help. Finally, I always keep notes that are made when there is time for some reflection and before my impressions get scrambled by other recollected gardens. Give yourself time and trust your instincts.'

Trevor Nottle, writer, Australia

'In the evening, Charlotte took him for a walk through the new parts of the garden. The captain took great pleasure in the countryside and admired all the fine views which the new paths set off to advantage. His eye was practised and yet easy to please; and although he could at times well imagine preferable solutions, he never awoke, as often happens, ill humour among those who were showing him their gardens by expecting more than circumstances might allow or by recalling what he had seen elsewhere that was even better.'

Johann Wolfgang von Goethe, *Elective Affinities*, 1809

COURTESY

What not to do
(The following are all real-life instances.)

Take exact measurements and detailed photographs so that you can reproduce a garden scene exactly at home. Especially if the garden owner makes his living designing gardens . . .

Browbeat the person selling tickets, and insist when she explains that she herself owns the garden: 'Oh you poor dear! all this is going to your head! I know who the real owners are, I saw them arrive by helicopter only last week!'

After an evening concert in a private château garden, walk off with a rugby ball belonging to the owners' young son. And reply, when challenged: 'People who open their gardens to the public should not leave their things lying around!'

Talk constantly to the owner who is showing you around about your own garden. Be where you are NOW, not far away.

Ask questions consistently just as someone else is starting to ask one of their own.

If the garden owner is a plant specialist, wail about your failures with that red geranium you bought at the supermarket.

Talk loudly about family problems, other gardens or favourite recipes, or conduct any private conversation while standing at the owner's elbow during the visit. If you are not interested, move away.

Wear bright colours, especially red, which will disturb other peoples' perceptions of the garden.

If the house is 'off limits', ask for the loo as an excuse to get inside, or peer through the windows.

Climb up on drystone walls to get a better picture and walk off leaving a crumbled wall behind you.

Make an appointment for four people and arrive with a group of ten.

Drop Kleenex or film packaging or any other debris about the garden for the owner to find later – and beware, such things can easily escape unobserved while you are rummaging for something else. If you are fussing around in your purse or camera bag, look behind you from time to time to make sure you have not been leaving a trail.

Give addresses of private gardens to all your friends – and strangers – without first checking with the owners.

Take cuttings without asking. Often owners are happy to give them to you.

Steal labels rather than writing down the names in the notebook you brought for that purpose (this and the stealing of cuttings is known as 'finger blight').

Keep asking the owner for the Latin names of rare plants, write them down, then pull up the plants and stuff them into a plastic bag as soon as she moves on. (Pat Jonas of the Brooklyn Botanic Garden discovered in *De Florum Cultura* of 1638 a warning from the author, Giovanni Battista Ferrari, that light-fingered gardeners will be turned into snails.)

'When visiting the garden of a person of a rank higher than one's own, a visitor must avoid praising it in too loud a voice.'

Japanese advice, 1200

What not to say
(Again, these are real-life instances.)

'When do you get flooooowwwers?'
'There are not enough flowers.'
'We're in a hurry, it will only take ten minutes.'
'When does it start looking good?'
'Is that plastic?'
'I have one of those too but mine's bigger.'
'I have one of those too, it spreads like wildfire!'
'Do you charge less when it's raining?'
'It's already late, can we pay less?'
'I guess you spend some time on this?'
'Or course with your soil, everything grows'

(said by visitors from Normandy to
   gardeners working with arid southern soil)
'Do you have to do anything or does it all just
   happen like that?' (a Parisian architect's
   question in the provinces)
'Too bad there are no palm trees.'
'I have that, and that, and that, and that, but hey,
   you don't have any begonias!'
'What's that scrubby bush over there?'
'What's making all that racket?' (of birdsong,
   or cicadas)
'Who were you trying to copy?'
'Is that real lawn?'
'Do you plant these things again every year?'
'Is THAT your garden?'
'If I were you, I'd have . . .'
'How to you expect me to know where to go
   without signposts?'
'Does all this belong to you?'
'Did you bring me all this way just to see THAT?'
   (said by a visitor to the friend who had
   brought him, in front of the owners)
'Oh, this is not at all like what they promised
   in Sunday's paper!' (especially if you are in
   the wrong garden . . .)

Said to Christopher Lloyd when he was
experimenting with his first wildflower
meadows: 'You don't know what a comfort it is
for a gardener like me to see weeds in a garden
like yours!' 'Did the owner die recently?' 'It's so
hard to get qualified help these days . . . ' 'It must
have been wonderful when it was kept up!'

One comment stands out as the most irritating to
owners: 'What is the best time to see this garden?'
It may seem the most natural question in the
world, but it implies that, whatever the best time
may be, it certainly isn't now. And furthermore
that there is ONE best time, whereas a garden has
many good moments. Often visitors simply mean,
when is the time with the most flowers ? but this
too is exasperating for owners who care a lot about
foliage, structure, perspectives, and so much more.

ADVICE TO OWNERS OPENING THEIR GARDENS FOR THE FIRST TIME

Groundwork

'I always advise owners about to open their
gardens to make up a management plan.
Gardeners are not always interested in finance but
you must be able to foresee the costs of upkeep
when you open your garden. Investing in new
creations is not the only expense. How much will
your lawn cost per square yard, how much your
beech hedge per foot, all those things. You need
to be very rigorous. In France the State will help
you restore or create a garden but no one gives
you subsidies for upkeep . . . Upkeep is essential. It
counts a good deal for us because our gardens are
formal and any slippage is immediately apparent,
especially when seen from above.'

Henri Carvallo, Château de Villandry, France

'If your garden is meant to have a natural look, or
if your budget and staff are too meagre, at the very
least rake the paths. This way visitors will know
you care.'

Benoît Bourdeau, garden designer, head gardener when
restoration began at Serre de la Madone, Menton,
on the French Riviera

'The success of a garden open to the public is 90
per cent upkeep, 10 per cent the original
conception.'

Arnaud Maurières, designer of many French public gardens

'Remember to wind up and hide the garden hoses
before the visitors arrive.

   If possible, get ready the day before, then
make a last tour to check forgotten details just
before they are due. Remember that visitors often
arrive before the scheduled time. Beware of last
minute improvements: fixing a water pipe just
before a wedding produced an unstoppable
geyser. The whole water network had to be turned
off and showers taken next door . . .'

George Brumder, garden owner and visitor, Pasadena, USA

Making appointments

Give clear directions and put up signposts if you can. Instead of 'a bit further along' give a rough figure in metres (or feet) or kilometres (or miles). Be sure you say 'left' for 'left' and 'right' for 'right'. Don't mention four landmarks at a turn-off when a single obvious one is enough. Give road and route numbers when possible. Check regularly that the signposts you mention are still in place and that route numbers have not changed.

Set a time convenient for you but make allowances for traffic conditions and have some patience for the lost wallets and misinterpreted directions that beleaguer most travellers at one time or another.

Taking people round

Make the ground rules clear: do you mind if people wander off on their own? If they take pictures for private use? You may prepare a brief introductory speech and then let people wander, or ask them to stay with you – or your guide – for the duration of the visit, but this should be clear from the start. People will wander unless otherwise directed, especially if your garden has appeared in the press and magazines.

Avoid walking at the front of a line and speaking into the air, or only to the few people immediately behind you. Find a place where everyone can gather and wait for the laggards to catch up. This will discourage those who disappear on their own and later come up and ask you to repeat what you have already explained several times. (There is no hope, however, for photographers, who must have pictures empty of people.)

'Give people a garden plan [in a big garden that is regularly open] so they can find their own way around, especially to the nursery, shop and loos. Different parts of the garden may be depicted with different colours or symbols but the whole thing should be easily readable. Why not suggest several possible itineraries? You can forbid certain

things such as the presence of domestic animals, but it is very unpleasant to visit a place with a long list of 'Don'ts'. Above all, be welcoming. Use visiting techniques adapted to the site and don't consider your visitors just a flock of sheep!'

Bill Malecki, garden advisor for the National Trust in England[8]

'To present a new garden to visitors, you should always give its historic context. If it is an old garden, be sure to mention both the past and future projects. If it is a private venture, discuss the circumstances of its creation, its possible ties with other works and wider movements, show how it is typical of its period. Don't neglect to mention the names of designers where their work made an important contribution. It is not enough just to walk around and point out plants.'

Maïté Delmas, distinguished botanist at the Jardin des Plantes in Paris and sometime garden tour guide

'You need to be consistent: if you decide to let people visit your garden and charge a fee for this, you need to make yourself available and welcoming and save enough energy to answer the many questions that will arise during the visit. For my part, I have three golden rules: never tell people certain places are off limits; never use a negative tone of voice; be as available as possible.'

Anne-Marie Deloire, owner of the Jardin des Fleurs de Poterie, on the French Riviera

'Don't laugh when a visitor asks the name of a common plant; don't answer "I've better things to do." Don't suggest that a garden (yours) is only as good as the wealth of its owners (yours).'

Serge and Brigitte Lapouge, owners of the Jardins de l'Albarède, Dordogne, France, and keen garden visitors

'Make yourself as available as possible and wear some outfit so striking that visitors will remember its originality. Receive each visitor as a unique, special person.'

Cléophée de Turckheim and Guillaume Pèlerin, owners of the Jardin Botanique de Vauville, Normandy, France

Richard Norman, a distinguished collector on the Riviera, once complained that all his visitors wanted was 'a drink and a pee'. Many garden visitors are seniors who have come a long way for visits. It is kind to provide both of these services. Visitors are then free to concentrate on what you have to show and say. Avoid saying, with a look of real concern: 'Oh, but if you use the loo, you'll be here so much longer!' You may wish to discourage visitors who ask for the loo just so they can get into the house: have one near the entrance door, or in the garden itself. Mediterranean gardens can usually offer a convenient pool house.

Signposting in the garden

If you use information panels or signposting, be imaginative as well as instructive. In France, top marks go to the Marqueyssac gardens in the Dordogne, to the Vallon du Villaret in the Lozère, and to the scenography of Rainer Verbizh at Vulcania, the scientific park and garden in the Auvergne.

'I keep thinking of Nori and Sandra Pope's sign in their (now derelict) garden at Hadspen: 'DONT PICK ANYTHING'. This definitely expresses the combination of codependence and suspicion that many gardeners feel towards visitors.'

Niall Hobhouse, owner of Hadspen Parabola Gardens, England

Most successful signpost in a private garden: 'You should have been here two weeks ago!'

A garden area with an evocative name immediately becomes much more tempting. Who would not want to see 'the Astronomers' Rendezvous' (at the Château du Vignal, near Nice)? The reality must not disappoint, however, once you get there. In some cases, the design process starts from a name at the outset: Patrick Charroy works with his team in the town of Cahors to create innovative gardens on abandoned town lots: 'We start from a name, imagine a theme, and then start flying!'

'We want an information panel that will provide a map and the names of different areas, the Poets' Rotunda, for example, but I don't want signposts. For me that means a public garden and we want ours to remain private, a private garden open to visitors, our guests.'

Madame de Pange, Château de Pange, Lorraine, France

Signposting does mark your garden as public, open to strangers, and this is a difficult bridge for many owners to cross: 'The more notices you put up,' said Christopher Lloyd, 'the less private and personal a garden becomes.'[9] At the Prieuré d'Orsan in France [p. 15], a daring project made by two passionate architects, Sonia Lesot and Patrice Taravella, which now receives about twenty thousand visitors yearly, the door of the loo remains unmarked, for this reason. Visitors must ask the ticket-sellers (who may be the owners) where to go . . .

Plant labelling

'Visitors love to be given the names of plants even if they forget them right away. The main thing is the act of naming.'

Henry Carvallo, Château de Villandry, France

'I feel my garden is still very much mine which I love to share with sympathetic gardeners. Often when I am a bit tired or depressed, a chance meeting with kindred spirits will revitalize me completely, but when I come across someone walking across a flower bed 'looking for a label', I can feel a sudden surge of rage and despair, as if they were trampling over me. The garden may be open, but it is not a public park, nor should public parks be treated with disrespect – please keep to the paths! Fortunately most people give us a lot of encouragement by their interest and appreciation of what we do.'

Beth Chatto, in correspondence with Christopher Lloyd[10]

Never label a rare plant until it has taken and spread, Christopher Lloyd advises.

Original solutions for gardens where labels are regularly stolen: use pieces of slate (too heavy to be carried off) or clothespins (easy to replace).

'I cannot complain about problems when I show my own garden. Visitors are usually considerate and if they do trample on a small treasure, well, the world does not come down. Yet it is clear to me that when 20 gardeners are expected, locations are chosen with wide paths or wilder areas, and also the group is kept moving. If I mean to "lecture," I always do so where sufficient space is available for everybody. On the other hand, when 1 or 2 accompany me, I often take them "cross country" on narrow paths. I have no set length for visits. If visitors are interested, the visit is delightful, if not I make it as short as possible. I have little patience with visitors who want to bend plants to their wishes, who want to grow all kinds of things that are not meant to thrive in a Mediterranean environment and to whom it never occurs that plants have their own predilections.

Visitors who constantly refer to their own garden make me wonder why they bothered to come. Or those who bombard me with "Que maravilla!," "Quelle merveille!," "A paradise!" Returning an ongoing compliment can be tiring.

After years in one's garden, one knows it so well that comments and creative criticism of others can turn out to be helpful. They may open one's eyes where habit has "blinded" us or blurred our view, and suddenly one may wonder why a particular aspect has not occurred to us before. Triggered by the visitor's suggestion or criticism, one may take the idea further and get even started on a new concept.'

Heidi Gildemeister, gardener and writer, Mallorca, Spain

A garden where we were made welcome.
    A garden with many different plants.
    A young garden.
    A garden in full flux.
    A garden once enjoyed in the rain.
    A garden that has once moved us.
    A fragrant garden.
    A beautiful garden!'

Eléonore Cruse, rose specialist, designer and owner of the Roseraie de Berty

NOTES

For details of publications, see Recommended Reading and Addresses.

Why Visit Gardens?

[1] Translated from the French, as given in Martine Vallette-Hémery, *Les Paradis naturels : jardins chinois en prose*, Arles 2001, p. 83.

[2] Richardson, *Avant Gardeners*, p. 312.

[3] Trinh Chi/CVN, 'Les paysans tirent profit des jardins touristiques', *Courrier du Vietnam*, 3 Dec. 2006.

[4] Bawa et al., *Lunuganga*, p. 240.

[5] For the history and a description of this remarkable place, see www.clt.astate.edu/elind/nc_main.htm, and www.rawvision.com/nekchand/nekchand. html

[6] A project of Kathryn Gustafson and partners.

[7] For Gardens Without Limits see www.jardins-sans-limites.com/site_engl. Quotations are from the Actes (minutes) of the 2004 and 2006 conferences in Metz.

[8] Actes, Metz, 2004, p. 23.

[9] 'Item' in *The Garden*, Sept. 2007, p. 574.

[10] Actes, Metz, 2004, p. 35.

[11] In *The Garden*, Sept. 2007, p. 583.

[12] For the history of Chaumont, see Jones, *Reinventing the Garden*.

[13] Quoted by Sally Charrett, *The Garden*, May 2007.

[14] Pigeat in *L'Esprit du japon* shows how the city of Nantes successfully adapted a public garden of Japanese inspiration to modern urban needs.

[15] *The Garden*, Dec. 2007.

[16] Lloyd, *In My Garden*, p. 177.

[17] Williams and Drew, *On Garden Style*.

[18] See www.jardinsambucs.com.

[19] Sitwell, *On the Making of Gardens*, p. 63.

[20] Richardson, essay on 'Nature' in *Avant Gardeners*, pp. 145–52.

[21] Quoted in Jones, *Reinventing the Garden*. See also Weller, *Room 4.1.3: Innovations in Landscape Architecture*.

[22] Hunt, foreword to Weilacher, *Between Landscape Architecture and Land Art*.

[23] Wareham, in articles quoted on the website of Veddw House, www.veddw.co.uk.

[24] See Lawrence Weschler and Betty Cohen, *Robert Irwin Getty Garden*, Los Angeles 2002, and www.getty.edu/visit/see_do/gardens.html

[25] Corinne Julius in *The Garden*, May 2007.

[26] Richardson, *Avant Gardeners*, pp. 33, 306, 308.

[27] See Richardson, *Avant Gardeners*, and www.ianhamiltonfinlay.com

[28] Quoted in Weilacher, *Between Landscape Architecture and Land Art*, p. 17. See also Jones, *Reinventing the Garden*.

[29] Cauquelin, *Petit Traité du jardin ordinaire*, Paris 2003, p. 128. See Jones, *New Gardens in Provence*.

[30] Peter Latz, on his participation in the Chaumont festival, quoted in Jones, *Reinventing the Garden*.

[31] Maurières, Ossart and Bouvier, *Jardins de voyage*.

[32] Waymark, *Modern Garden Design*, pp. 6–7.

[33] See many books by the French gardener Gilles Clément, especially *Une Ecologie humaniste*, written in collaboration with Louisa Jones.

[34] Actes, Metz, 2004, p 15.

[35] From the website www.latzundpartner.de.

[36] Quoted in Jones, *Reinventing the Garden*. See also Weller, *Room 4.1.3: Innovations in Landscape Architecture*.

[37] Tamura, *Art of the Landscape Garden in Japan*, p. 7.

[38] Actes, Metz, 2004, p 45.

[39] The digest of several surveys, published in *Télérama*, 25 July 2007, no. 3002.

[40] Dossier de presse, Ministère de la Culture, distributed for the Garden Open weekend, 2005.

[41] For Picardy see the website www.baiedesomme.fr.

[42] See the website of the Comité Départemental de Tourisme of the Gard department, with a downloadable garden brochure and itinerary: www.tourismegard.com.

[43] A major theme of the conference at Metz in 2006.

[44] Page, *The Education of a Gardener*, p. 172.

Ten Questions for Ten Styles . . .

[1] Page, *The Education of a Gardener*, p. 50.

[2] Labourdette, 'Enjeux pour la réhabilitation d'un jardin historique: Rénovation, restauration ou recréation', Séminaire du Château de Barbirey, Sept. 2003; colloquium papers available on www.barbirey.com. The ICOMOS-IFLA International Committee for Historic Gardens, meeting in Florence on 21 May 1981, decided to draw up a charter on the preservation of historic gardens which would bear the name of that town. The present Florence Charter was drafted by the Committee and registered by ICOMOS on 15 Dec. 1982. The Charter defines the historic garden as 'an architectural and horticultural composition of interest to the public from the historical or artistic point of view'. The full text is available on the website: www.international.icomos.org/e_floren.htm.

[3] The gardens of Valloires were recreated by Gilles Clément, Alnwick by Wirtz International.

[4] Baridon, *Les Jardins*, intro., p. 5.

[5] Sitwell, *On the Making of Gardens*, p. 82.

[6] Wharton, *Italian Villas and their Gardens*, p. 6.

[7] Colette, *La Vagabonde*, 1910, trans. Enid MacLeod as *The Vagabond*, New York 1955, pp. 192–93.

[8] Françoise Crémel, garden architect, with Elisabeth Lemercier and Louise de Constantin, architects, for the Chokelao Palace Garden in Jodhpur: project presentation in *Patrimoine (jardins) & Création contemporaine*, Enghien-les-Bains 2006.

[9] Actes, Metz, 2004, p. 19.

[10] First published in *Lettres édifiantes et curieuses écrites des missions étrangères par quelques missionnaires de la compagnie de Jésus*, Paris 1749, 27: 1–61. This translation, by Joseph Spence (alias Sir Harry Beaumont), was published in London in 1752.

[11] Francis and Hester, eds, *The Meaning of Gardens*, pp. 120–30.

[12] Quoted in Scott-James, *The Language of the Garden*, p. 73.

[13] Page, *The Education of a Gardener*, p 15.

[14] Anne Scott-James, *The Cottage Garden*.

[15] A famous phrase used by Vita Sackville West in a seminal article, 'Hidcote Manor', in *Journal of the Royal Horticultural Society*, vol. 74, no. 11, Nov. 1949, pp. 476–81. This appreciation was partly responsible for the confusion and overlapping of the Arts and Crafts and the cottage style, though Sackville West did not confuse them.

[16] Lassus, *Couleur, lumière, paysage: instants d'une pédagogie*, Paris 2004, pp. 115–16.

[17] Nicole Arboireau, author of *Jardins de grands-mères*, spent a lot of time finding just the right electric blue for her own garden props.

[18] Colette, *Sido*, Paris 1901, p. 12.

[19] Anne Scott-James reminds us that the 'Fairy' rose owes its very survival to its popularity in cottage gardens.

[20] Quoted in Kathleen Bronzert and Bruce Sherwin, eds, *The Glory of the Garden*, New York 1993, p. 68.

[21] Elizabeth von Arnim tells the story in *Elizabeth and her German Garden*, 1898 (a classic, many editions available).

[22] Lassus, *Couleur, lumière, paysage* (cit. at n. 16 above), p. 115.

[23] See Jones, *The French Country Garden*.

[24] Arboireau, *Jardins de grands-mères*, p. 44.

[25] Scott-James, *The Cottage Garden*, p. 27.

[26] Rousseau, *Julie, or the New Heloise*: letter XI to Milord Edward, pp. 387ff.

[27] Arboireau, *Jardins de grands-mères*, pp. 12–13.

[28] Hallé, *In Praise of Plants*.

[29] Li Yu, transl. from the French, 'La Demeure et son jardin', as given in Martine Vallette-Hémery, *Les Paradis naturels: jardins chinois en prose*, Arles 2001, p. 139.

[30] Demoly and Picard, *Guide du Patrimoine botanique en France*.

[31] Moore, Mitchell and Turnbull, *The Poetics of Gardens*.

[32] Demoly and Picard, *Guide du Patrimoine botanique en France*, intro.

[33] Ill. in Filippi, *The Dry Gardening Handbook*.

[34] Results quoted by Patrick Taylor in 'The World's Most Influential Gardens', *The Garden*, May 2006, p. 320. The study was Biodiversity in Urban Gardens, or BUGS, carried out by the University of Sheffield.

[35] English transl. by Louisa Jones, from the French transl. of 1929 by Joseph Gagnaire.

[36] In a lecture given at the 4th European Landscape Architecture Biennale, Barcelona, March 2006.

[37] Montaigne, *Essais*, I, 31, Paris 1939, p. 102.

[38] Colette, *Break of Day*, transl. by Enid McLeod, New York 1961, p. 79.

[39] Cueco, *Dialogue avec mon jardinier*, pp. 66–67.

40 Jean-Baptiste de La Quintinie, *Instructions pour les jardins fruitiers et potagers*, 1690, transl. in 1693 by John Evelyn as *The Compleat Gard'ner*, p. 21.

41 Robinson, *The Parks and Gardens of Paris: Being Notes on a Study of Paris Gardens*, 2nd edn, rev., London 1878, p. 462.

42 Serres, *Le Théâtre de l'agriculture*.

43 Quoted on chef Dan Barber's home page at Stone Barns, www.bluehillstonebarns.com/bhsb.html. See also www.stonebarnscenter.org.

44 Danielle Dagenais, 'Cucul la sculpture?', *Le Devoir*, 4 Aug. 1995, repr. in *Côté Jardin*, Montreal 1997, p. 245.

45 Walker and Simo, *Invisible Gardens*, p. 84.

46 Stevens, 'Anecdote of the Jar', 1919:

I placed a jar in Tennessee,
And round it was, upon a hill.
It made the slovenly wilderness
Surround that hill.

The wilderness rose up to it,
And sprawled around, no longer wild.
The jar was round upon the ground
And tall and of a port in air.

It took dominion everywhere.
The jar was gray and bare.
It did not give of bird or bush,
Like nothing else in Tennessee.

47 Walker and Simo, *Invisible Gardens*, p. 84.

48 Richardson, *Avant Gardeners*, p. 33.

49 This account was taken from the Barbirey website: www.barbirey.com .

50 Goldsworthy, in the original project statement of 1999. See *Andy Goldsworthy, Refuges d'art*, and the website: www.musee-gassendi.org.

51 Cauquelin, *Petit Traité du jardin ordinaire*, p. 119.

52 ibid., p. 128.

53 Raxworthy, in a lecture given at the 4th European Landscape Architecture Biennale, Barcelona, March 2006.

54 See many examples in Jones, *New Gardens in Provence*.

55 Sontag, *On Photography*, New York 1977, p. 130: 'It was photography that first put into circulation the idea of an art that is produced not by pregnancy and childbirth but by a blind date (Duchamp's theory of 'rendez-vous')'. Cf. Anne Cauquelin, *Petit Traité d'art contemporain*, Paris 1996, p. 135: 'La rencontre de cet objet naturel participe de l'aventure, du hasard, d'un rendez-vous aléatoire, souvent éphémère.'

56 See Jones, *Reinventing the Garden*.

57 Lassus, *Couleur, lumière, paysage* (cit. at n. 16 above), p. 24.

58 Long, *Walking in Circles*, London 1991, quoted in Weilacher, *Between Landscape Architecture and Land Art*, p. 16.

59 See Clément and Jones, *Une écologie humaniste*.

60 Waymark, *Modern Garden Design*, p. 98.

61 Goldsworthy, *Time*, after p. 22.

63 Clément 'L'Art dépend de la cuisson', in *Où en est l'herbe?*.

63 Robinson, *The Parks and Gardens of Paris: Being Notes on a Study of Paris Gardens*, 2nd edn, rev., London 1878, p. 22.

64 Clément and Jones, *Une Ecologie humaniste*, p. 13.

65 See Hunt, *The Picturesque Garden in Europe*.

66 Nigel Dunnett, 'Artistic Ecology', *The Garden*, May 2004, p. 359. See also many other articles and books by Nigel Dunnett and Noel Kingsbury.

67 Page, *The Education of a Gardener*, p. 184: 'If you are a garden designer you can scarcely be a purist since a garden is by definition an artifice. To try to imitate nature exactly, just as to fly in her face, leads to absurdity. When you plant trees and shrubs, however informally, your aim is to intensify a natural ambience and to condense and underline a theme derived form nature herself'.

68 See Hunt, *Greater Perfections*.

69 Robson, *Bawa*.

70 See Gildemeister's books, *Mediterranean Gardening* and *Gardening the Mediterranean Way*.

71 Oase Foundation, co-ordinated by Willy Leufgen and Marianne van Lier, cited by Nigel Dunnett in 'Artistic Ecology', *The Garden*, May 2004, p. 358.

72 'Ma spécificité est d'être relié au vivant': interview with Emmanuel de Roux, *Le Monde*, 11 Aug. 2005.

73 Quoted in Brown, *The Modern Garden*, p. 87.

74 Proceedings of the Colloquium at the Brooklyn Botanic Gardens, 'Native plants: towards a 21st century garden, frontiers of ecological design' and 'Native plants: necessary or not?', 1997.

75 Clément and Jones, *Une Ecologie humaniste*, p. 18.

76 See many articles in *The Garden* by Isabelle van Groeningen, Nigel Dunnett and Brita von Schoenaich, books by Noel Kingsbury, Henk Gerritsen, Piet Oudolf, etc.

77 Gerritsen, *The Ecology of the Garden*, forthcoming book.

78 Clément and Jones, *Une Ecologie humaniste*, p. 79: this is a quotation from notes prepared by Clément for the English journalist Jane Thomas in relation to the article 'The Garden in Motion', *Garden Design Journal*, May 2005, pp. 37-40.

79 Kingsbury, 'As the Garden, so the earth: the politics of the "natural" garden', in Kingsbury and Richardson, eds, *Vista: the Culture and Politics of the Garden*.

80 Rousseau, *Julie, or the New Heloise*, pp. 388-93.

81 Mabey, introduction to Robinson, *The Wild Garden*, London 1983.

82 Quoted from www.veddw.co.uk.

83 From *Wood and Garden*, quoted in Kathleen Bronzert and Bruch Sherwin, eds, *The Glory of the Garden*, New York 1993, p. 37.

84 Williams and Drew, *On Garden Style*, p. 34.

85 McCoy, *Michael McCoy's Garden*, p. 8. He adds: 'I began to look at the garden through the eyes of those seeing it for the first time,

removing all the emotional associations of plants given as gifts … I analysed it, as if unaware of all the experiences that have brought me to this point, all the garden prejudices, my many horticultural strengths and outrageous weaknesses, my family's needs and my own, personal needs from my living-spaces. I began to look at it and think of it at times in a narrow, one-dimensional way, as if it were nothing more than a visual experience.'

86 Mitchell, *One Man's Garden*, p. 106.

87 Bennett, *Our Gardens Ourselves*, pp. 4–5.

88 Virgil, *Georgics*, quoted in Bennett, *Our Gardens Ourselves*, p. 10.

89 *Garden Design Journal*, no. 66, Dec. 2007, p 46. See also the website, www.thehadspenparabola.com, and the shortlisted designs on display at the Museum of Garden History, www.museumgardenhistory.org.

90 In the phrase of designer Ian Kitson.

91 Quoted on the website of Veddw House, www.veddw.co.uk .

92 Cauquelin, *Petit Traité du jardin ordinaire*, p. 167.

93 Mitchell, *The Essential Earthman*, pp. 135–36.

94 Bowers, in the audio anthology *The Writer in the Garden*, produced and directed by Jane Garmey, High Bridge Company, Saint Paul, Minn., 1996.

95 Anne Scott-James, *Gardening Letters to my Daughter*, p. 43.

96 Durrell, 'Across Secret Provence', in *Spirit of Place*, pp. 356–57.

97 Papanek, *The Green Imperative*, p. 118.

98 Pliny's several gardens are described in the *Epistulae*.

99 Boccaccio, *The Decameron*, trans. G. H. McWilliam, Harmondsworth, Mx, 1972, p. 592.

110 Wharton, *Italian Villas and their Gardens*, p. 19.

101 Fitzgerald, *Tender is the Night* (first pub. 1933), New York 1986, pp. 23–24.

102 Caruncho, quoted in Cooper and Taylor, *Gardens for the Future*, p. 178.

103 See books by Heidi Gildemeister and Olivier Filippi.

104 Durrell, in Maria Polushkin Robbins, ed., *The Cook's Quotation Book: A Literary Feast*, Wainscott, N.Y. 1975, p 77: 'The whole Mediterranean, the sculpture, the palms, the gold beads, the bearded heroes, the wine, the ideas, the ships, the moonlight, the winged gorgons, the bronze men, the philosophers – all of it seems to rise in the sour, pungent smell of these black olives between the teeth. A taste older than meat, older than wine. A taste as old as cold water.'

105 Caruncho, in Cooper and Taylor, eds, *Mirrors of Paradise*, p. 15.

106 Virgil, 'Le Petit Jardin', in *Bucoliques, Géorgiques, Catalectes*, Paris 1980, p. 197.

107 Tamura, in *Art of the Landscape Garden in Japan* (dedicated to members of the Garden Club of America in commemoration of their visit to Japan in 1935), p. 10.

108 Barthes, *L'Empire des signes*, Paris 1970, p. 102.

109 Tamura, *Art of the Landscape Garden in Japan*, p. 5.

110 ibid., p. 10, and Junichiro Tanizaki, *In Praise of Shadow*.

111 Baridon, *Les Jardins*, pp. 467, 492.

112 Tamura, *Art of the Landscape Garden in Japan*, p. 10.

113 Tanizaki, *In Praise of Shadow*, p. 53, reproaches Western culture with the introduction of electricity, bright, white-tiled bathrooms, shiny glass instead of paper windows, and more such 'sunny openness'.

114 Tamura, *Art of the Landscape Garden in Japan*, p. 5.

115 This can be metonymy – a part for the whole – or metaphor, one thing standing for another.

116 Tamura, *Art of the Landscape Garden in Japan*, p. 38. He prefers these to Western 'lawn-and-walk' gardens.

117 'In scarcely any instance of Japanese architecture is the house made so predominant as to overshadow the significance of the garden.' Tamura, *Art of the Landscape Garden in Japan*, p. 65.

118 Pigeat, *L'Esprit du japon dans nos jardins*, p. 96, notes that a closed gate in Japan is not 'a refusal to admittance but an invitation to mystery'.

119 Tamura, *Art of the Landscape Garden in Japan*, p. 63

120 Pigeat, pp. 56, 72.

121 Tamura, *Art of the Landscape Garden in Japan*, p. 12.

122 ibid., p. 68

123 Pearson recounted some of his experiences in Japan at the Association of Professional Landscape Designers US–British meetings at Kew Gardens in 2004. He also mentioned the difficulties in encouraging visitors to run their fingers through plants, and his need to respect customs such as placing seats side-by-side, never face-to-face.

124 Tamura, *Art of the Landscape Garden in Japan*, pp. 7–8, writes: 'In Japan, plants are so various in kind and so delicate in reacting to changes of season and circumstance that, in the budding, colouring, and fading, peculiar to each kind, they exquisitely tell the gradual cycle of the year".

125 Baridon, p. 473.

126 See a long description in Tamura, *Art of the Landscape Garden in Japan*, pp. 61ff.

127 Serra, 'Interview with Lynne Cook', in *Writings, Interviews*, p. 253, quoted by William J. R. Curtis in Laurie A. Stein, ed., 'The Pulitzer Foundation for the Arts: Tadao Ando, Ellsworth Kelly, Richard Serra Essay', St Louis 2001.

128 Tanizaki, p. 76.

129 Walker and Simo, *Invisible Gardens*, p. 56, n. 1.

130 Quoted by Curtis, cit. at n. 127.

131 Editorial in *The Garden*, Sept. 2002, p. 677.

132 Quoted from their website, www.latzundpartner.de. See also Weilacher, *The Syntax of Landscape: The Landscape Architecture of Peter Latz and Partners*.

133 Preface to Cooper and Taylor, *Mirrors of Paradise: the Gardens of Fernando Caruncho*.

134 Many of whom simply discount the post-modern parenthesis of the 1970s and 1980s.

135 This vocabulary – gesture, the power of the worked surface, and seriality – comes from Peter Walker with Cathy Deino Blake, 'Minimalist Gardens without Walls' in Francis and Hester, eds, *The Meaning of Gardens*, pp. 120–30.

136 Mies van der Rohe, 1959, widely quoted, for example in Christopher Bradley Hole, *The Minimalist Garden*, London 2000, p. 6.

137 From the titles of their books: Thomas Church and Grace Hall, *Gardens are for People*, first pub. 1955; Garrett Eckbo, *Landscape for Living*, first pub. 1950 .

138 See Richardson, *Avant Gardeners*, and Walker and Simo, *Invisible Gardens*, 'The Garden as Social Vision', pp. 30–56.

139 Aaron Betsky, 'The Long and Winding Path', preface to Amidon, *Moving Horizons: The Landscape Architecture of Kathryn Gustafson and partners*, p. 7.

140 For these three contrasting examples see Brown, *The Modern Garden*.

141 Courajoud, quoted in many places, among them Marielle Hucliez, *Jardins et parcs contemporains*, Paris 1998, p. 13.

142 See Brown, *The Modern Garden*, Masterwork Four, p. 100.

143 Quoted in Walker and Simo, *Invisible Gardens*, p. 99.

144 Quoted in Brown, *The Modern Garden*, p. 10.

145 Page, *The Education of a Gardener*, p. 266

146 Eckbo, quoted in Brown, *The Modern Garden*, p. 86.

147 See Jones, *New Gardens in Provence* Stewart, Tabori and Chang, 2006, ch. 16.

148 Brown, *The Modern Garden*, p. 194.

149 Lassus, *Couleur, lumière, paysage* (cit. at n. 16 above).

150 Walker, cit. at n. 135, pp. 120–30.

151 Contemporary designer Mark Rios insists: 'Pure Modernism is devoid of the concept of site - its expression comes out of the way things are pieced together. Our work is the opposite: we use the sense of place. It comes out of a connection with memory, the place and the culture. Our work tries to turn up the volume on experience.' Quoted in Richardson, *Avant Gardeners*.

152 Brown, *The Modern Garden*, p. 200.

153 Walker and Simo, *Invisible Gardens*, p. 172.

154 Richardson, *Avant Gardeners*, p. 38.

155 In 'Three Conversations with Andy Goldsworthy'.

156 Quoted in Jones, *Reinventing the Garden*. See Weller, *Room 4.1.3: Innovations in Landscape Architecture*.

Advice from the Wise

1 Scott-James, 'Garden Open Today', in *Gardening Letters to My Daughter*, p. 39

2 Lloyd, *In My Garden*, pp. 171–72. This book has a whole chapter called 'Visit an English Garden'.

3 Russell Page, p. 173

4 Lloyd, *In My Garden*, p. 36.

5 Nottle, *Gardens of the Sun*, p.67.

6 ibid.

7 Chatto and Lloyd, *Dear Friend and Gardener*, p. 113.

8 Actes, Metz, 2004.

9 Lloyd, *In My Garden*, p.166. When people began discovering and misunderstanding his meadows, his brother and sister-in-law suggest putting up a notice explaining rough grass to visitors, with a list of wild flowers, season by season, suggesting what to look for. His reply: 'Shan't.'

10 Chatto and Lloyd, *Dear Friend and Gardener*, p. 95.

RECOMMENDED READING

Amidon, Jane *Moving Horizons: The Landscape Architecture of Kathryn Gustafson and partners*, Basel/Boston, Mass., 2005

Andrews, R. *Maya Lin: Systematic Landscapes*, New Haven/London 2006

Anisko, Tomasz *Plant Exploration for Longwood Gardens*, Portland, Ore., 2006

Arboireau, Nicole *Jardins de grand-mères*, Aix-en-Provence 1999

Arnim, Elizabeth von *Elizabeth and her German Garden*, London 2006 (first pub. 1898)

Baridon, Michel *Les Jardins: paysagistes, jardiniers, poètes*, Paris 1998

Barthes, Roland *L'Empire des signes*, Paris 1970

Bawa, Geoffrey, Christophe Bon and Dominic Sansoni, *Lunuganga*, London 2006

Bennett, Jennifer *Our Gardens Ourselves*, London 1994

Borja, Erik *Zen Gardens: Space and Illusion* London 2000

Bradley Hole, Christopher *The Minimalist Garden*, London 2000

Brookes, John *The Essentials of Garden Design*, New York 2008

—— *Room Outside: A New Approach to Garden Design*, London 1979, repr. 2007

—— *The Well-Designed Garden*, London 2002

Brown, Jane *The Modern Garden*, London 2006

—— *The Pursuit of Paradise: A Social History of Gardens and Gardening*, London 2006

Cabot, Francis H. *The Greater Perfection: The Story of the Gardens at Les Quatre Vents*, New York 2001

Cauquelin, Anne *Petit Traité du jardin ordinaire*, Paris 2003

Chatto, Beth, and Christopher Lloyd *Dear Friend and Gardener: Letters on Life and Gardening*, London 1998

Church, Thomas, and Grace Hall *Gardens are for People*, Berkeley, Calif., 1995 (first pub. 1955)

Clément, Gilles *Où en est l'herbe? Réflexions sur le jardin planétaire*, ed. Louisa Jones, Arles 2006

——, and Louisa Jones *Une Ecologie humaniste*, Paris 2006

—— Cooper, Guy, and Gordon Taylor, in *Gardens for the Future*, London 2000

—— *Mirrors of Paradise: the Gardens of Fernando Caruncho*, London 2000, p. 15

Cooper, Paul *Gardens Without Boundaries*, London 2003

Cueco, Henri *Dialogue avec mon jardinier*, Paris 2000, pp. 66–67

Dagenais, Danielle *Côté Jardin*, Montreal 1997

Danneyrolles, Jean Luc *Le Jardin extraordinaire*, Arles 2001

Dillon, Helen *Helen Dillon's Garden Book*, London 2007

Demoly, Jean-Pierre, and Franklin Picard *Guide du patrimoine botanique en France*, Arles 2005

Dronet, Thierry and Monique *Le Jardin de Berchigranges*, Paris 2008

Durrell, Lawrence *Spirit of Place: Letters and Essays on Travel*, ed. Alan G. Thomas, New Haven 1969

Duus, Masayo *The Life of Isamu Noguchi: Journey Without Borders*, Princeton, N.J., 2006

Filippi, Olivier *The Dry Gardening Handbook: Plants and Practices for a Changing Climate*, London 2008

Ford, Ford Madox *Provence*, New York 1979 (first pub. 1935)

Francis, Mark, and Randolph T. Hester, eds *The Meaning of Gardens* Cambridge, Mass., 1991

Gerritsen, Henk *Henk Gerritsen – An Essay on Gardening*, Amsterdam 2009

——, and Piet Oudolf *Planting the Natural Garden*, Portland, Ore., 2003

Gildemeister, Heidi *Gardening the Mediterranean Way: Practical Solutions for Summer-dry Climates*, London 2006

—— *Mediterranean Gardening: A Waterwise Approach*, Palma de Mallorca 1995

Goldsworthy, Andy *Time*, London 2000

—— *Andy Goldsworthy, Refuges d'art*, Digne 2002

—— 'Three Conversations with Andy Goldsworthy': conversation with John Fowles, in Terry Friedman and Andy Goldsworthy, eds, *Hand to Earth: Andy Goldsworthy Sculpture 1976–1990*, New York 1990, p. 162

Hallé, Francis *In Praise of Plants*, Portland, Ore., 2002

Hill, Penelope *Contemporary History of Garden Design: European Gardens Between Art And Architecture*, Princeton, N.J., 2004

Hobhouse, Penelope *In Search of Paradise: Great Gardens of the World*, London 2006

—— *Plants in Garden History*, London 2004

—— *The Story of Gardening*, London 2002

Hucliez, Marielle *Jardins et parcs contemporains*, Paris 1998

Hunt, John Dixon *Greater Perfections*, London 2000

—— *The Picturesque Garden in Europe*, London 2002

Johnstone, Lesley, ed. *Hybrids: Reshaping the Contemporary Garden in Métis*, Vancouver 2007

Jones, Louisa *La Bambouseraie*, Arles 2003

—— *The French Country Garden*, London 2000

—— *New Gardens in Provence*, New York 2006

—— *Reinventing the Garden: Global Inspirations from the Loire*, London 2003

Kingsbury, Noël 'As the Garden, so the earth: the politics of the "natural" garden', in

Noel Kingsbury and Tim Richardson, eds, *Vista: the Culture and Politics of the Garden*, London 2005

Lassus, Bernard *The Landscape Approach*, Philadelphia, Pa., 1998

Lloyd, Christopher *Cuttings: A Year in the Garden with Christopher Lloyd*, London 2007

—— *In My Garden*, ed. Frank Ronan, London 1994

—— *The Well Tempered Garden*. London 2003

Malpas, William *The Art of Andy Goldsworthy: Complete Works* (special edn), Maidstone, Kt, 2007

Maurières, Arnaud, and Eric Ossart *Paradise Gardens: Landscape Gardening in the Islamic Tradition*, London 2001

—— *Les Jardins de Ossart & Maurières*, Paris 2008

—— and Lionel Bouvier *Jardins de voyage: 20 leçons de paysage*, Aix-en-Provence 2007

McCoy, Michael *Michael McCoy's Garden*, Glebe, Australia, 2000

Mitchell, Henry *One Man's Garden*, New York 1992

—— *The Essential Earthman*, New York 1981

Moore, Charles W., William J. Mitchell and William Turnbull, Jr *The Poetics of Gardens*, Cambridge, Mass., n.d.

Nottle, Trevor *Gardens of the Sun*, Portland, Ore., 1996

Quest-Ritson, Charles *The Gardens of Europe: A Traveller's Guide*, Woodbridge, Suff., 2007

Page, Russell *The Education of a Gardener*, Harmondsworth, Mx., 1985

Papanek, Victor *The Green Imperative: Ecology and Ethics in Design and Architecture*, London 1995

Pigeat, Jean-Paul *L'Esprit du japon dans nos jardins*, Paris 2006

Richardson, Tim *Avant Gardeners: Fifty Visionaries of the Contemporary Landscape* London 2008

—— *English Gardens of the Twentieth Century: From the Archives of 'Country Life'*, London 2005

——, ed. *The Garden Book*, London 2005

Robinson, William *The Parks and Gardens of Paris: Being Notes on a Study of Paris Gardens*, 2nd edn, rev., London 1878

—— *The Wild Garden*, London 1983 (first pub. 1870)

Robson, David *Bawa: Geoffrey Bawa: the Complete Works*, London 2002

Rousseau, Jean-Jacques *Julie, or the New Heloise*, transl. and annotated by Phillip Stewart and Jean Vaché, Hanover/London 1997

Saunders, William S., ed. *Richard Haag: Bloedel Reserve and Gas Works Park*, Princeton, N.J., 1999

Schwartz, Martha, and Tim Richardson *The Vanguard Landscapes and Gardens of Martha Schwartz*, London 2004

Scott-James, Anne *The Cottage Garden*, Harmondsworth, Mx., 1981

—— *Gardening Letters to my Daughter*, New York 1991

—— *The Language of the Garden: A Personal Anthology*, Harmondsworth, Mx., 1987

Serres, Olivier de *Le Théâtre de l'agriculture*, Arles 1997 (first pub. 1600)

Simms, Barbara *John Brookes, Garden and Landscape Designer*, London 2007

Sitwell, George *On the Making of Gardens*, Boston, Mass., 2004

Spencer-Jones, Rae *1001 Gardens You Must See Before You Die*, London 2007

Strong, Roy *Gardens Through the Ages*, London 2000

—— *The Laskett*, London 2003

Tamura, Tsuyoshi *Art of the Landscape Garden in Japan*, Tokyo 1935

Tanizaki, Junichiro *In Praise of Shadow*, transl. Edward G. Seidensticker, New Haven 1977

Taylor, Patrick, ed. *The Oxford Companion to the Garden*, Oxford 2006

Vallette-Hémery, Martine *Les Paradis naturels : jardins chinois en prose*, Arles 2001

Walker, Peter, and Melanie Simo, *Invisible Gardens: The Search for Modernism in the American Landscape*, Cambridge, Mass., 1992

Walton, Susana *The Mortella: an Italian Garden Paradise*, London 2002

Wareham, Anne Articles quoted on the website of Veddw House, www.veddw.co.uk

Waymark, Janet *Modern Garden Design: Innovation since 1900*, London 2003

Weilacher, Udo *Between Landscape Architecture and Land Art*, Basel 1996

—— *The Syntax of Landscape: The Landscape Architecture of Peter Latz and Partners*, Basel 2007

Weller, Richard *Room 4.1.3: Innovations in Landscape Architecture*, Philadelphia, Pa., 2005

Weschler, Lawrence, and Betty Cohen *Robert Irwin Getty Garden*, Los Angeles 2002

Wharton, Edith *Italian Villas and their Gardens*, Cambridge, Mass./New York 1976 (first pub. 1904)

Wijaya, Made *Modern Tropical Garden Design*, London 2007

—— *Tropical Garden Design*, London 2003

Williams, Bunny, and Nancy Drew, *On Garden Style*, New York 1998

ADDRESSES OF GARDENS, DESIGNERS, AND OTHER EXPERTS

AUSTRALIA
Garden of Australian Dreams
National Museum of Australia
Lawson Crescent, Acton Peninsula, Canberra,
ACT 2600
Postal address: GPO Box 1901, Canberra,
ACT 2601
Tel. +61 2 6208 5000 Fax +61 2 6208 5099
www.nma.gov.au/index.html
Heronswood Gardens
105 Latrobe Parade
Dromana, 3936 Melways (near Melbourne)
Tel. +61 3 5984 7900 Fax +61 3 5987 2398
www.diggers.com.au
Karkalla Gardens (Fiona Brockhoff)
Landscape Design Office:
10 Keating Avenue, Sorrento, VIC 3943
Tel. +61 3 5984 4282
Gardens: Mornington Peninsula
www.opengarden.org.au
Wigandia (William Martin)
PO Box 46, Noorat, VIC 3265
www.wigandia.com

BALI
Made Wijaya, designer
www.ptwijaya.com

BELGIUM
Wirtz International, designers
(Jacques, Peter, Martin)
Botermelkdijk 464, B-2900 Schoten
Tel. +32 3 680 13 22 Fax +32 3 680 13 23
www.wirtznv.be/Femke1.htm

BRAZIL
Sítio Roberto Burle Marx
administered by the IPHAN
(Instituto do Patrimônio Histórico e Artístico
Nacional/Ministério da Cultura), Barra de
Guaratiba, Estrada de Guaratiba 2019,
Rio de Janeiro 23020-240
Tel. +55 21 2410 1412
www.mapwing.com/explore/
view_tour.php?t=MQfdKWoKoRfddddd

CANADA
**Jardins de Métis/Reford Gardens and
International Garden Festival**
200, route 132, Grand-Métis (Quebec),
GOJ 1ZO
Tel. +1 418 775 2222 Fax +1 418 775-6201
Les Quatre Vents (Francis H. Cabot)
accessible through the Centre écologique de
Port-au-Saumon, 3330 boulevard Malcolm-
Fraser (route 138), La Malbaie (Quebec)
G5A 2J5
Tel. +1 877 434 2209 Fax +1 418 434 2559
cepas@charlevoix.net
www.cepas.qc.ca/jardin.php

CHILE
Juan Grimm
juangrimm@terra.cl

FRANCE
Jardins d' Agapanthe (Alexandre Thomas)
76850 Grigneuseville (Normandy)
Tel. +33 2 35 33 32 05 Fax +33 2 35 33 48 86
www.jardins-agapanthe.fr
Jardins de l'Albarède (Serge Lapouge and
Brigitte Lapouge-Déjean)
24250 Saint-Cybranet (Dordogne)
Tel. +33 5 53 28 38 91
jardins.albarede@wanadoo.fr
www.jardins-albarede.com
Jardin de l'Alchimiste
13810 Eygalières (Provence)
Tel. +33 4 90 90 67 67 Fax +33 4 90 95 99 21
www.jardin-alchimiste.com
ALEP, designers
La Glaneuse, Avenue Philippe-de-Girard,
84160 Cadenet (Provence)
Tel. +33 4 90 68 88 84 Fax +33 4 90 68 88 85
contact@alep-paysages.com
www.alep-paysage.com
Jardin d'Anne-Marie (Anne-Marie Grivas)
2 rue 8 mai 1945, 91510 Lardy (near Paris)
Tel. +33 1 60 82 30 63
Bambouseraie de Prafrance (Muriel Nègre)
Générargues, 30140 Anduze (Languedoc)
Tel. +33 4 66 61 70 47 Fax +33 4 66 61 64 15
www.bambouseraie.fr
Jardins de Barbirey (Véronique and
Jean-Bernard Guyonnaud)
2 rue du Château, 21410 Barbirey-sur-Ouche
(Burgundy)
Tel. +33 3 80 49 08 81 Fax +33 3 80 49 08 81
www.barbirey.com
Bayol Gallery (Doudou and Joseph Bayol)
Quartier Plantier Major,
13210 Saint-Rémy-de-Provence
Tel./Fax +33 4 90 92 11 97
www.josephbayol.com
Berchigranges (Thierry and Monique Dronet)
9 route du Tholy, 88640 Granges-sur-Vologne
(Lorraine)
Tel. +33 3 29 51 47 19
www.berchigranges.com
Carrières de Bibémus
Office de Tourisme d'Aix-en-Provence
2 place du Général-de-Gaulle,
13100 Aix-en-Provence
Tel. +33 4 42 16 11 61
www.aixenprovencetourism.com
Bitche Citadel festival garden
Gardens Without Limits
Présidence, Conseil Général de la Moselle,
1 rue du pont Moreau, 57000 Metz
Tel. +33 3 87 35 01 00
pascal.garbe@cg57.fr
www.jardins-sans-limites.com/site_engl/
index.htm
Patrick Blanc, designer
www.verticalgardenpatrickblanc.com
Bois des Moutiers (Mallet family)
76119 Varengeville (Normandy)
Tel. +33 2 35 85 10 02
Fax +33 2 35 85 46 98
www.gardenvisit.com/garden/
les_bois_des_moutiers, or
www.chateaux-france.com/boisdesmoutiers

Erik Borja, designer
Les Clermonts, 26600 Beaumont-Monteux
(Rhône)
Tel./Fax : +33 4 75 07 32 27
erik.borja@hotmail.fr
Jardins Secrets, Cahors
Office de Tourisme, Place F. Mitterrand,
46000 Cahors
Tel. +33 5 65 53 20 65 Fax +33 5 65 53 20 74
officetourisme@mairiecahors.fr
www.mairie-cahors.fr/Tourisme/
page-anglais.html
Le Cerf (restaurant, Husser family)
30 rue du Général de Gaulle,
67520 Marlenheim (Alsace)
Tel. +33 3 88 87 73 73 Fax +33 3 88 87 68 08
www.lecerf.com
**Chaumont-sur-Loire: Conservatoire
International des Parcs et Jardins et du
Paysage**
Ferme du Château, 41150 Chaumont-sur-Loire
Tel. +33 2 54 20 99 22 Fax +33 2 54 20 99 24
www.chaumont-jardins.com
Gilles Clément, designer
www.gillesclement.com
Jardins Clos de la Forge
(Christian Allaert and Jacques Sautot)
Crozant, 23160 Villejoint (Limousin)
Tel. +33 5 55 89 82 59 / +33 5 55 89 83 64
Le Clos du Pioule (Nicole Jalla-Cervlei)
07260 Dompnac (Rhône)
Tel. +33 4 75 36 95 54
Cordes-sur-Ciel: Jardin des Paradis
Place du Théron, 81170 Cordes-sur-Ciel
(Midi-Pyrénées)
Tel. +33 5 63 56 29 77 Fax +33 5 63 56 23 32
www.cordes-sur-ciel.org
Domaine de Courson (Fustier family)
91680 Courson Montloup (near Paris)
Tel. +33 1 64 58 90 12 Fax +33 1 64 58 97 00
www.domaine-de-courson.fr
Muriel de Curel see Château de Saint-Jean-
de-Beauregard
Olivier Filippi / Pépinières Filippi
RN 113, 34140 Mèze (Languedoc)
Tel. +33 4 67 43 88 69 Fax +33 4 67 43 84 59
www.jardin-sec.com
Jardin des Fleurs de Poterie
(Anne-Marie Deloire)
250 Chemin des Espeiroures, 06510 Gattières
(Riviera)
Tel./Fax +33 4 93 08 67 77
homepage.mac.com/jardindepoterie
Stéphane Gaillacq, consulting gardener
Tel. +33 2 47 50 42 68
stephane.gaillacq@orange.fr
Giverny (Musée Claude Monet)
84 rue Claude Monet, 27620 Giverny
(Normandy)
Tel. +33 2 32 51 28 21
www.fondation-monet.com/uk/informations
Andy Goldsworthy (works by A.G. and
other sculptors)
Musée Gassendi (curator Nadine Gomez-
Passamar)
64 boulevard Gassendi, 04000 Digne-les-Bains
(Provence)

Tel. +33 4 92 31 45 29 Fax +33 4 92 32 38 64 and Cairn (Centre d'art informel et de recherche sur la nature)
www.musee-gassendi.org, and www.refugesart.org
Dominique Lafourcade, designer
10 Boulevard Victor Hugo,
13210 Saint-Rémy-de-Provence
Tel. +33 4 90 92 10 14 Fax +33 4 90 92 49 72
www.architecture-lafourcade.com
Laquenexy Orchard
Gardens Without Limits
Présidence, Conseil Général de la Moselle
1 rue du Pont Moreau, 57000 Metz
Tel. +33 3 87 35 01 00
pascal.garbe@cg57.fr
www.jardins-sans-limites.com/site_engl/index.htm
La Louve (Nicole de Vésian)
Judith Pillsbury, 84480 Bonnieux (Provence)
jinfrance@aol.com
Jardins du Manoir d'Eyrignac
24590 Salignac (Dordogne)
Tel. +33 5 53 28 99 71 Fax +33 5 53 30 39 89
www.eyrignac.com
Jardins de Marqueysac
24220 Vezac (Dordogne)
Tel. +33 5 53 31 36 36 Fax +33 5 53 31 36 30
www.marqueyssac.com
Pépinières Maymou (Paul Maymou nursery)
Chemin Moulin Habas, 64100 Bayonne (Aquitaine)
Tel. +33 5 59 55 05 24 Fax +33 5 59 50 16 52
pepinieres.maymou@orange.fr
Jardin des Mille et une Fleurs
(Maria-Grazia et Bruno Cancelli)
Les Abris, 30760 Saint-Julien-de-Peyrolas (Rhône)
Tel. +33 6 88 08 31 55
Camille Muller, designer
211 rue du Faubourg Saint-Antoine, 75011 Paris
Tel. +33 1 43 67 46 95
www.camillemuller.com
Marc Nucera, plant sculptor
BP 16, 13550 Noves (Provence)
Tel./Fax +33 4 90 92 99 21
Prieuré d'Orsan (Patrice Taravella)
18170 Maisonnais (Loire)
Tel. +33 2 48 56 27 50 Fax 33 2 48 56 39 64
www.prieuredorsan.com
Ossart & Maurières SARL, designers
2 rue Henri-Drussy, 41000 Blois
Tel. +33 2 54 55 06 37 Fax +33 2 54 58 92 53
ossart-maurieres@wanadoo.fr
Hugues Peuvergne, designer
42bis avenue du Général Leclerc,
77400 Lagny-sur-Marne (near Paris)
Tel./Fax +33 1 64 30 61 75
hugues.peuvergne@wanadoo.fr
Jardin Plume (Sylvie and Patrick Quibel)
76116 Auzouville-sur-Ry (Normandy)
Tel./Fax +33 2 35 23 00 01
www.lejardinplume.com
Jardins de la Pomme d'Ambre
(Nicole Arboireau)
Impasse ancienne route d'Italie, La Tour-de-Mare, 83600 Fréjus (Riviera)

Tel. +33 4 94 53 25 47 Fax +33 4 94 52 95 50
www.gardeninprovence.com/frnicole.html
Pépinières Jean Rey
La Pascalette, RD 559
83250 La Londe-les-Maures (Provence Riviera)
Tel. +33 4 94 00 41 00
www.jeanrey.fr
Château de Saint-Jean-de-Beauregard
(M. and Mme de Curel)
91940 Les Ulis (near Paris)
Tel. +33 1 60 12 00 01 Fax +33 1 60 12 56 31
www.domsaintjeanbeauregard.com
Erik Samakh, artist
samakh@club-internet.fr
Jardin des Sambucs
(Agnès and Nicholas Brückin)
Le Villaret, 30570 Saint-André-de-Majencoules (Languedoc)
Tel. +33 4 67 82 46 47 / +33 6 82 49 59 19
www.jardinsambucs.com
Arborétum de la Sédelle (Philippe and Nell Wanty)
Crozant, 23160 Villejoint (Limousin)
Tel. +33 5 55 89 84 44
Michel Semini , designer
Rue Saint Frusquin, 84220 Goult (Provence)
Tel. +33 4 90 72 38 50 Fax +33 4 90 72 38 52
Serre de la Madone
74 Route de Gorbio, 06500 Menton (Riviera)
Tel. +33 4 93 57 73 90 Fax +33 4 93 28 55 42
www.serredelamadone.com
Terre Vivante
Domaine de Raud, 38710 Mens (Alps)
Tel. +33 4 76 34 80 80 Fax 33 4 76 34 84 02
www.terrevivante.org
Jardins de Valloires, including Lamarck Gardens
80120 Argoules (Picardy)
Tel. +33 3 22 23 53 55 Fax +33 3 22 23 91 32
www.jardins-de-valloires.com
Château de Valmer (Mme de Saint-Venant)
37210 Chançay (Loire)
Tel. +33 2 47 52 93 12 Fax +33 2 47 52 26 92
www.chateau-de-valmer.com
Château de Vaux le Vicomte
77950 Maincy (near Paris)
Tel. +33 1 64 14 41 90 Fax +33 1 60 69 90 85
www.vaux-le-vicomte.com/visites-chateau.php
Château de Versailles
78000 Versailles
Tel. +33 1 30 84 74 00
www.chateauversailles.fr
Château de Villandry
37510 Villandry (Loire)
Tel. +33 2 47 50 02 09 Fax +33 2 47 50 12 85
www.chateauvillandry.com
Vallon du Villaret (Guillaume Sonnet)
48190 Bagnols-les-Bains (Lozère)
Tel. +33 4 66 47 63 76 Fax +33 4 66 47 63 83
www.levallon.fr

GERMANY
Herrenhausen
Informations-Pavillon der Herrenhäuser Gärten, Herrenhäuser Straße 4,
30419 Hannover
Tel. +49 511 1684 7743 / +49 511 1684 7374
www.hannover.de/herrenhausen/index.html or

www.niedersachsen-tourism.de/en/regionen-staedte/staedte/hannover/herrenhausen-gardens/index.php
Latz and Partners
(Peter, Anneliese and Tilman Latz), designers
LandschaftsArchitekten / Planer BDLA, OAi Lux
Ampertshausen 6, D-85402 Kranzberg
Tel. +49 81 6667 8519 Fax +49 81 6667 8533
www.latzundpartner.de
Blumeninsel Mainau (Gräfin Sonja Bernadotte)
Abteilung Servicezentrum, D-78465 Insel Mainau (Lake Constance)
Tel. +49 75 31 303 0 Fax +49 75 31 303 248
www.mainau.de
Westpark
(designer Rosemarie Weisse)
Untersendling, Pressburger Strasse, 80539 Munich
www.muenchen.de

GREECE
Cali Doxiadis, journalist and garden owner in Corfu
mgspastpresident4@gmail.com

INDIA
Nek Chand's Rock Garden at Chandigarh
Nek Chand Foundation in the UK, 1 Watford Road, Radlett, Herts, WD7 8LA
Tel. +44 1923 856644
www.nekchand.com

IRAN
Bagh-e Shahzadeh
Mahan, Kerman

IRELAND
Ballymaloe Cookery School
Shanagarry, Co. Cork
Tel. +353 21 4646785 Fax +353 21 4646909
cookingisfun.ie/pages/our_gardens
The Dillon Garden (Helen Dillon)
45 Sanford Road, Ranelagh, Dublin 6
www.dillongarden.com

ISRAEL
Garden of Gethsemane
Mount of Olives, Kidron Valley,
City of Jerusalem

ITALY
Villa Cetinale
53018 Soviculle (near Siena)
Tel. +39 0577 311 147
www.villacetinale.com
Villa d'Este
Piazza Trento 5, 00019 Tivoli (Rome)
Tel. +39 0424 600 460
(ticket office) +39 0774 332 920
Fax +39 0424 464 191
www.villadestetivoli.info/indexe.htm
Villa Gamberaia
Via del Rossellino 72, 50135 Settignano (Florence)
Tel. +39 055 697 205 / 055 697 090 Fax +39 055 697 090
villagam@tin.it
www.villagamberaia.com

Giardini Hanbury (Hanbury Botanical Gardens)
Corso Montecarlo 43,
18038 La Mortola Inferiore, Ventimiglia-Latte
Tel. +39 0184 229 507
www.amicihanbury.com
Isola Bella
Lago Maggiore, Piemonte
www.borromeoturismo.it, or
www.lagomaggiore.net/old/uk/citta/I-Bella.asp
LAND-I Landscape Architects
Antonini Capecci Sini
Via Madonna dei Monti 50, 00184 Rome
Tel.+39 064 746 782 Fax +39 064 828 525
www.archicolture.com
Villa Lante
Bagnaia (near Viterbo), Lazio
Tel. +39 0761 288 008
info@bagnaia.vt.it
La Mortella
Via Francesco Calise 39, 80075 Forio,
Isola d'Ischia, Napoli
Tel. +39 081 986 220 Fax 081 986 237
www.lamortella.it
Giardini e Rovine di Ninfa
04010 Doganella di Ninfa, Lazio
Tel. +39 0773 633 935
www.fondazionecaetani.org/ninfa/
ninf_home.htm
Contessa Giuppi Pietromarchi
La Ferriera, 58011 Capalbio, Grosseto
Tel. +39 0564 895 046 Fax +39 0564 895 123
giuppi.pietromarchi@tin.it

JAPAN
Daigo-ji 22 Higashi Oji-cho
27 Monguchi-cho, Ishojo-ji, Sakyo-ku,
Kyoto-shi, Kyoto-hu
www.daigoji.or.jp/e
Heian Jingu
Sakyo-ku, Okazaki Nishi, Tenno-cho,
Kyoto-shi, Kyoto-hu
Kamigamo-jinja Shinto Shrine (Kamo-wake
ikazuchi Jinja)
339 Motoyama, Kamigamo, Kita-ku, 603-8047
Tel. +81 75 781 0011 Fax +81 75 702 6618
www.kamigamojinja.jp/english/index-e.html
Marunouchi Hotel
Pacific Century Place, 1-11-1 Marunouchi,
Chiyoda-ku, Tokyo 100-6277
Tel. +81 3 5222 7222
www.fourseasons.com/marunouchi
Ryoan-ji Temple
Ukyo-ku, Ryoanji, Goryoshita-cho,
Kyoto-shi, Kyoto-hu
Saiho-ji Temple
Nishigyo-ku, Matsuo, Kamigatani-cho,
Kyoto-shi, Kyoto-hu
Tel. +81 75 391 3631
Sesshu-in Temple (also Funda-in, Sesshuin)
Higashiyama-ku, Honmachi, 15-chome,
Kyoto-shi, Kyoto-hu
Shisen-do Hall
27 Monguchi-cho Ichijoji, Sakyo-ku,
Kyoto-shi, Kyoto-hu
Tel. +81 75 781 2954
Taizo-in Temple
Ukyo-ku, Hanazono, Myoshinji-cho,
Kyoto-shi, Kyoto-hu

Fumiaki Takano, designer
1-37 Nishi Aza-Mannen Otofuke-Cho,
Katou-Gun, Hokkaido
Tel. +81 155 42 3181 Fax +81 155 42 3863
www.tlp.co.jp
Tofuku-ji Temple
Higashiyama-ku, Honmachi, 15-chome,
Kyoto-shi, Kyoto-hu

MEXICO
Jose de Yturbe
Monte Caucaso no. 915, 5th Floor,
Lomas de Chapultepec
Tel. +52 55 5284 5000 Fax +52 55 5284 5001

NETHERLANDS
Huis Bingerden
Bingerdenseweg 21, 6986 CE Angerlo
Tel. +31 31 348 28 24 Fax +31 31 347 55 73
www.bingerden.com
Henk Gerritsen *see* Priona
Paleis Het Loo Nationaal Museum
Koninklijk Park 1, 7315 JA Apeldoorn
www.paleishetloo.nl
Priona (Henk Gerritsen)
Schuineslootweg 13, 7777 RE Schuinesloot
(near Slagharen)
Tel. +31 52 368 17 34 Fax +31 52 368 27 97
www.prionatuinen.com/priona-web/
menu-eng.html
Arboretum Trompenburg (Riet Van Hoey
Smith, former director)
Honingerdijk 86, 3062 Rotterdam
Tel. +31 10 233 01 66 Fax +31 10 233 01 71
arboretum@trompenburg.nl

NEW ZEALAND
Ted Smyth, landscape architect and artist
Tel. +64 9 810 9697
landspirit@xtra.co.nz

NORWAY
Vigeland Sculpture Park
City of Oslo, Agency for Cultural Affairs
and Sports Facilities, Vigeland Museum,
Postboks 1453 Vika, 0116 Oslo
Tel. +47 23 49 37 00 Fax +47 23 49 37 01
www.museumsnett.no/vigelandmuseet/
2parken/2b_historikk/engelsk

SOUTH AFRICA
Brenthurst Gardens
PO Box 1050, Houghton, Johannesburg, 2041
Tel. +27 11 646 4122 Fax +27 11 646 1529
www.brenthurstgardens.co.za/
welcome.php?section=gardens
Kirstenbosch
National Botanical Garden of South Africa
Postal address: Rhodes Drive, Newlands
Private Bag X7, Claremont
Tel. +27 21 799 8899 Fax +27 21 797 6570
Information office: +27 21 799 8783
www.sanbi.org/frames/kirstfram.htm
Stellenberg (Sandy Ovenstone)
Oak Avenue, Kenilworth, Cape Town
Visits by appointment with the plant nursery
Tel. +27 21 761 2948

Rustenberg Estate
PO Box 33, Stellenbosch 7599
Tel. +27 21 809 1200 Fax. +27 21 809 1219
www.rustenberg.co.za

SPAIN
Alhambra and Generalife Gardens
18009 Granada
www.alhambradegranada.org, or
www.alhambra.org/eng
Fernando Caruncho & Asociados, S.L.,
designers
Paseo de Narcea, 17
Urbanización Ciudalcampo, 28707 Madrid
Tel. +34 91 657 00 51 Fax +34 91 657 02 80
www.fernandocaruncho.com
Beth Galí Studio, designers
www.bethgali.com
César Manrique Foundation
Taro de Tahiche, Lanzarote, Canary Islands
Tel. +34 928 84 31 38 / +34 928 84 30 70
Fax +34 928 84 34 63
www.fcmanrique.org
Fundació Jardí Botànic de Sóller
(Botanical Garden of Soller)
Apartat de Correus 44, E-07100 Sóller, Mallorca
Tel. +34 971 63 40 14 Fax +34 971 63 47 81
www.jardibotanicdesoller.org/eng/
index.html

SRI LANKA
Lunuganga (now a hotel)
The Sun House, Dedduwa Lake, Bentota
Tel. +94 91 4380275 Fax +94 91 2222624
info@thesunhouse.com
www.lunuganga.net

SWEDEN
Japanese Gardens in Brunnspark, Ronneby
Contact Tony Åhlund, Town Hall, Ronneby
Tel. +46 457 187 30
www.ronneby.se
Woodland Cemetery/Skogskyrkogården
www.stockholm.se/skogskyrkogarden

THAILAND
Jim Thompson House
6 Soi Kasemsan 2, Rama 1 Road, Bangkok
Tel. +66 2 216 7368
Fax +66 2 612 3744
www.jimthompsonhouse.com

UNITED KINGDOM
Alnwick Castle
Alnwick, Northumb., NE66 1YU
Tel. +44 1665 511350 Fax +44 1665 511351
www.alnwickgarden.com
Barnsley House (formerly Rosemary Verey's,
now a hotel)
Cirencester, Glos., GL7 5EE
Tel. +44 1285 740000
www.barnsleyhouse.com
Biddulph Grange
Grange Road, Biddulph, Staffs., ST8 7SD
Tel. +44 1782 517999
www.nationaltrust.org.uk

John Brookes *see* Denmans Gardens
Beth Chatto Gardens
Elmstead Market, Colchester, Essex, CO7 7DB
Tel. +44 1206 822007
www.bethchatto.co.uk
Denmans Gardens
(John Brookes, designer, and Joyce Robinson)
Denmans Lane, Fontwell, W. Sussex, BN18 0SU
Tel. +44 1243 542808 Fax +44 1243 544064
www.denmans-garden.co.uk
East Lambrook Manor (Margery Fish)
South Petherton, Som., TA13 5HH
Tel. +44 1460 240328 Fax +44 1460 242344
www.eastlambrook.co.uk
Great Dixter (Christopher Lloyd)
Northiam, Rye, E. Sussex, TN31 6PH
Office: Tel. +44 1797 252878 Fax +44 1797 252879
Nursery: Tel. +44 1797 253107
www.greatdixter.co.uk
Tony Heywood, designer
Room B200, Macmillan House, Platform One,
Paddington Station, London, W2 1FT
Tel. +44 20 7402 6884
www.conceptualgardens.co.uk
Hidcote Manor Garden
Hidcote Bartrim, Glos., GL55 6LR
Tel. +44 1386 438333
www.nationaltrust.org.uk
Penelope Hobhouse, designer and author
www.penelopehobhouse.com
Inverewe Garden
Poolewe, Ross and Cromarty, Scotland, IV22 2LG
inverewe@nts.org.uk
www.nts.org.uk
Royal Botanic Gardens, Kew
Richmond, Surrey, TW9 3AB
Tel. +44 20 8332 5655
www.kew.org
Lady Farm (Judy Pearce)
Chelwood, Som., BS39 4NN
Tel. +44 1761 490770
www.ladyfarm.com
Little Sparta (Ian Hamilton Finlay)
Stonypath, Dunsyre, near Lanark, Lanarks.,
Scotland ML11 8NG
Little Sparta Trust (Laura Robertson)
Tel. +44 7826 495677
little_sparta@btinternet.com
www.littlesparta.co.uk
Le Manoir aux Quat' Saisons (Raymond Blanc)
Church Road, Great Milton, Oxon., OX44 7PD
Tel. +44 1844 278881 Fax +44 1844 278847
www.manoir.com
Mount Stewart House and Garden
Greyabbey, Newtonwards, Northern Ireland,
BT22 2AD
Tel. +44 2842 788387 Fax +44 2842 788569
www.nationaltrust.org.uk
Dan Pearson Studio
80c Battersea Rise, London SW11 1EH
Tel. +44 20 7924 2518 Fax +44 20 7924 2523
www.danpearsonstudio.com/index_02.html
**Pensthorpe Millennium Gardens and
Wildlife Reserve**
Fakenham Road, Fakenham, Norf., NR21 0LN
Fax +44 1328 855905
www.pensthorpe.com/location.htm

Hannah Peschar Sculpture Garden
Black and White Cottage
Standon Lane, Ockley, Surrey, RH5 5QR
Tel. +44 1306 627269 Fax +44 1306 627662
www.hannahpescharsculpture.com
Tim Rees, designer
Trees Associates
www.treesassociates.com
Garden Organic Ryton
Coventry, Warw., CV8 3LG
Tel. +44 24 7630 3517 Fax +44 24 7663 9229
www.gardenorganic.org.uk
Sissinghurst Castle Garden
Cranbrook, Kent, TN17 2AB
www.nationaltrust.org.uk
Stowe Landscape Gardens
near Buckingham, Bucks., MK18 5DQ
Tel. +44 1494 755568
www.nationaltrust.org.uk
Julie Toll Landscape & Garden Design
Business & Technology Centre, Bessemer
Drive, Stevenage, Herts., SG1 2DX
Tel. +44 1438 310095 Fax +44 1438 310096
www.julietoll.co.uk
Tresco Abbey Gardens (Robert Dorrien-Smith)
Isles of Scilly
Tel. +44 1720 424108 Fax +44 1720 422868
mikenelhams@tresco.co.uk
www.tresco.co.uk/stay/abbey-garden
Veddw House
(Anne Wareham and Charles Hawes)
Devauden, Mon., Wales, NP16 6PH
Tel. +44 1291 650836 Fax +44 1291 650948
www.veddw.co.uk
West Green House Gardens (Marylyn Abbott)
near Hartley Wintney, Hook, Hants, RG27 8JB
Tel. +44 1252 844611 / 1252 845582
Fax +44 1252 842029
www.westgreenhouse.co.uk

USA
Ruth Bancroft Garden
1552 Bancroft Road, Walnut Creek, CA 94598
Tel. +1 925 944 9352 Fax +1 925 256 1889
www.ruthbancroftgarden.org
Bloedel Reserve (designer Richard Haag)
7571 NE Dolphin Drive, Bainbridge Island,
WA 98110
Tel. +1 206 842 7631 Fax +1 206 842 8970
www.bloedelreserve.org
Chanticleer Garden
786 Church Road, Wayne, PA
Tel. +1 610 687 4163
www.chanticleergarden.org
Topher Delaney, designer
600 Illinois Street, San Francisco, CA 94107
Tel. +1 415 621 9899 Fax +1 415 626 8998
tdelaney@tdelaney.com
Filoli
86 Cañada Road, Woodside, CA 94062
Tel. +1 650 364 8300, ext. 507 Fax +1 650 367 0724
tours@filoli.org
www.filoli.org
Isabelle Greene & Associates, designer
2613 De La Vina Street, Santa Barbara, CA 93105
Tel. +1 805 569 4045 Fax +1 805 569 2270
iga@isabellegreene.com

Gustafson Guthrie Nichol Ltd, designers
Pier 55, Floor 3, 1101 Alaskan Way, Seattle,
WA 98101
Tel. +1 206 903 6802 Fax +1 206 903 6804
www.ggnltd.com
in Britain: **Gustafson Porter Landscape**
www.gustafson-porter.com
Richard Haag & Associates Inc.
Landscape Architects
2412 10th Avenue East, Seattle, WA 98102
Tel. +1 206 325 8119 Fax +1 206 325 8722
rhaag@richhaagassoc.com
www.richhaagassoc.com
John P. Humes Japanese Stroll Garden
347 Oyster Bay Road, Locust Valley, NY 11560
Tel. +1 516 676 4486
www.locustvalley.com/japanese%20stroll%20
garden.html
Huntington Botanical Gardens
1151 Oxford Road, San Marino, CA 91108
Tel. +1 626 405 2100
www.huntington.org
Innisfree Gardens
Millbrook, NY 12545
Tel +1 845 677 8000
www.innisfreegarden.org
Jungles Landscape Architect, designer
242 SW 5th Street, Miami, FL 33130
Tel. +1 305 858 6777 Fax +1 305 856 0742
www.raymondjungles.com
Maya Ying Lin
Maya Lin Studio, 112 Prince Street, New York,
New York 10012
Tel. +1 212 941 6463 Fax +1 212 941 6464
MLinStudio@aol.com
Longwood Gardens
1001 Longwood Road, Kennett Square , PA 19348
Tel. (information) +1 610 388 1000
www.longwoodgardens.org
Lotusland Foundation
695 Ashley Road, Santa Barbara, CA 93108
Tel. (reception) +1 805 969 3767,
(reservations) +1 805 969 9990 Fax +1 805 969 4423
www.lotusland.org/visitor.html
Lurie Garden (Gustafson Guthrie Nichol Ltd,
Piet Oudolf and Robert Israel)
Millennium Park, 201 E. Randolph Street,
Chicago, IL 60601
Tel. +1 312 742 1168
www.millenniumpark
Steve Martino & Associates, designer
111 East Dunlap Avenue, Suite 1-625, Phoenix,
AZ 85020
Tel. +1 602 957 6150 Fax +1 602 224 5288
www.stevemartino.net
Naumkeag
Reservations through the Trustees
The Mission House
PO Box 792, Sergeant Street, Stockbridge, MA
01262
Tel. +1 413 298-3239
www.berkshireweb.com/trustees/naumkeag.html
Noguchi Museum
32–37 Vernon Boulevard, Long Island City,
NY 11106
Tel. +1 718 204 7088 Fax +1 718 278 2348
www.noguchi.org

Norton Simon Museum of Art
(gardens designed by Nancy Goslee Power)
411 W. Colorado Boulevard, Pasadena,
CA 91105-1825
Tel. +1 626 449 6840
www.nortonsimon.org/visitor.aspx
Our Own Stuff Gallery-Garden
Artwork by Mark Bulwinkle and Marcia
Donahue
3017 Wheeler Street, Berkeley, CA
web.mac.com/markbulwinkle/Bulwinkleland/
Garden.html, and
www.literate-lemur.com/gallery2
Japanese Garden in Portland
PO Box 3847, Portland, OR 97208-3847
Tel. +1 503 223 1321 Fax +1 503 223 8303
www.japanesegarden.com
Nancy Goslee Power and Associates
www.nancypower.com
Elizabeth Scholz, emeritus director,
Tour Office
Brooklyn Botanic Gardens, 1000 Washington
Avenue, Brooklyn, NY 11225-1099
Tel. +1 718 623 7239
touroffice@bbg.org
www.bbg.org
Martha Schwartz, Inc., designer
147 Sherman St., Suite 200, Cambridge,
MA 02140
Tel. +1 617 661 8141 Fax +1 617 661 8707
www.marthaschwartz.com
Blue Hill at Stone Barns (restaurant)
630 Bedford Road, Pocantico Hills,
NY 10591
Tel. +1 914 366 9600
www.bluehillstonebarns.com
Vietnam Veterans Memorial
Postal address: Operations/Vietnam Veterans
Memorial, National Park Service, National
Capitol Parks-Central, 900 Ohio Drive, S.W.,
Washington, DC 20242
Tel. +1 202 426 6841 / +1 202 619 7225
thewall-usa.com

VIETNAM
Garden-Tomb of the Emperor Tu Duc
outside Hué Central
www.vietnamtourism.com/Hue/e_pages/
lt_ltuduc.htm

SOURCES OF ILLUSTRATIONS

a: above; b: below

page 1 Louisa Jones; **2** Courtesy of Heidi Gildemeister; **8** Dominic Sansoni/ThreeBlindMen; **11** Julia Elmore, Raw Vision/The Nek Chand Foundation; **12** Courtesy of Mainau GmbH; **13** Andrea Jones/Garden Exposures Photo Library; **15** Allan Pollock-Morris; 17, 19 Louisa Jones; **24–25** Andrea Jones/Garden Exposures Photo Library; **27** Courtesy of Latz + Partner; **30** Jerry Harpur/Harpur Garden Images; 35 Louisa Jones; **39, 40** Andrea Jones/Garden Exposures Photo Library; **41a** Jerry Harpur/Harpur Garden Images; **41b** Andrea Jones/Garden Exposures Photo Library; **42, 43** Andrew Lawson; **44** Courtesy of Vigeland Museet og Parken, Oslo; **45a** Charles Hawes; **45b** Philippe Perdereau; **46, 47b** Jerry Harpur/Harpur Garden Images; **47a** Louisa Jones; **48** Andrew Lawson; **49** Andrea Jones/Garden Exposures Photo Library; **51** Andrew Lawson; **52** Christopher Bradley-Hole/Clive Nichols; **54** Jerry Harpur/Harpur Garden Images; **55** Louisa Jones; **56** Philippe Perdereau; **57** John Glover; 59, 60, 62 Louisa Jones; **63** Camille Muller/Louisa Jones; 64, 65 Henk Gerritsen/ The Priona Gardens, The Netherlands; **66** Courtesy of Jardin des Paradis, Cordes-sur-Ciel; 67, 68 Louisa Jones; **70** Photo by Nicolas Havette, Land Art by Mireille Fulpis/La Bambouseraie, Domaine de Prafrance; **71** Jerry Harpur/Harpur Garden Images; **73** Andrea Jones/Garden Exposures Photo Library; **74** Jerry Harpur/Harpur Garden Images; **75** John Glover; 76, 77, 79 Jerry Harpur/Harpur Garden Images; **80a** Clive Nichols; **80b** Andrea Jones/Garden Exposures Photo Library; **81** Louise Thomas; **82** Andrea Jones/Garden Exposures Photo Library; **83** Jean-Pierre Delagarde/Château de Courson; **84** Allan Pollock-Morris; **86, 87** Vincent Motte/Louisa Jones; **88** Allan Pollock-Morris; **89** Louisa Jones; **90, 91** Jerry Harpur/Harpur Garden Images; **92** Allan Pollock-Morris; **93** Andrew Lawson; **94** Jen Munkvold, Los Angeles; **95** Courtesy of Le Manoir aux Quat' Saisons, Oxford; **96** Jerry Harpur/Harpur Garden Images; **97** Courtesy of Pascal Garbe/Gardens Without Limits; **98** Courtesy of Garden Organic; **99** Louisa Jones; **100** Jerry Harpur/Harpur Garden Images; **102** César Manrique/Clive Nichols; **103** Louisa Jones; **104** Allan Pollock-Morris; **105** Andrew Lawson; **106** Louisa Jones; **107** Sophie Ryder/Hannah Peschar Gallery/Clive Nichols; **108** Andrea Jones/Garden Exposures Photo Library; **109** Louisa Jones; **110** Andrea Jones/Garden Exposures Photo Library; **111** Louisa Jones; **112** Jerry Harpur/Harpur Garden Images; **113, 115, 116** Louisa Jones; **118** Andrew Lawson; **119** Allan Pollock-Morris; **120** Andrea Jones/Garden Exposures Photo Library; **121** Courtesy of Nicola Browne/Dan Pearson Studios; **122** Andrea Jones/Garden Exposures Photo Library; **123** Louisa Jones; **125** Charles Hawes;

126–27 Andrea Jones/Garden Exposures Photo Library; **128** Courtesy of Willem Hardijzer/Brenthurst Gardens, Johannesburg; **129** Philippe Perdereau; **130, 131** Louisa Jones; **132, 134** Jerry Harpur/Harpur Garden Images; **135** Louisa Jones; **136** Hans Fonk/Courtesy of the James H. W. Foundation, Bangkok; **137** Allan Pollock-Morris; **138** Louisa Jones; **139** Helen Dillon; **140** Jerry Harpur/ Harpur Garden Images; **141** Charles Hawes; **142** Jerry Harpur/Harpur Garden Images; **143** Philippe Perdereau; **144** Louisa Jones; **145** Clive Nichols; **147** Allan Pollock-Morris; **148** Laurie Hégo; **150** Louisa Jones; **151** Philippe Perdereau; **153** Jerry Harpur/Harpur Garden Images; **154, 156, 157** Louisa Jones; **158–59a** Andrea Jones/Garden Exposures Photo Library; **159b** Marcus Harpur/Harpur Garden Images; **160** Jerry Harpur/Harpur Garden Images; **161** Clive Nichols; **162** Courtesy of Heidi Gildemeister; **163** Louisa Jones; **164** Courtesy of Olivier Filippi/Pépinière Filippi; **166** Japan Travel Bureau/Photolibrary; **167** Andrea Jones/Garden Exposures Photo Library; **168, 169** Japan Travel Bureau/ Photolibrary; **170** Tohoku/Getty Images; **171** Japan Travel Bureau/Photolibrary; **172** B.S.P.I./Corbis; **173** Jerry Harpur/Harpur Garden Images; **174a** Philippe Perdereau; **174b** DAJ/Getty Images; **176** Michael Jenner, Robert Harding Travel/Photolibrary; **177** Japan Travel Bureau/Photolibrary; **178–79** Andrea Jones/Garden Exposures Photo Library; **180a** Clive Nichols; **180b** Ken Straiton/Getty Images; **182, 183** Jerry Harpur/Harpur Garden Images; **184** Clive Nichols; **185** Jerry Harpur/ Harpur Garden Images; **186** Andrea Jones/ Garden Exposures Photo Library; **187, 188** Jerry Harpur/Harpur Garden Images; **189** Clive Nichols; **191–93** Jerry Harpur/Harpur Garden Images; **194–95** Andrea Jones/Garden Exposures Photo Library; **196** Architectural Design/De Yturbe Arquitectos, Mexico. Photo Fernando Cordero; **201** Harpur Garden Images/Corbis; **202, 204, 207** Jerry Harpur/Harpur Garden Images; **208** Paul Prescott/Alamy; **211** FAN travelstock/Alamy; **213** Andrea Jones/Garden Exposures Photo Library; **214** Michael S. Yamashita/Corbis; **216** Panoramic Images/Getty Images; **217** John Ferro Sims/Garden Picture Library/Photolibrary; **218** Edward Diestelkamp; **220** Kenneth Garrett, National Geographic/Getty Images; **223** David Lyon/Alamy; **224–25a** Andrea Jones/Garden Exposures Photo Library; **224–25b** The Irish Image Collection/Photolibrary; **227** Andrew Lawson/Alamy; **228** Andrea Jones/Garden Exposures Photo Library; **229** Dave Bartruff/ Corbis; **230** Kevin Lang/Alamy; **233** Edward Diestelkamp.
The drawings on pages 1, 3–7, 36–37, 198–99 and 234–35 are by Drazen Tomic.

INDEX

Numbers in **bold** type refer to illustrations and to information in captions, indexed by the page on which the illustration – not the caption – falls